PLACE NAMES
of the WHITE
MOUNTAINS

Julyan, Robert and Mary
Place Names of the White Mountains

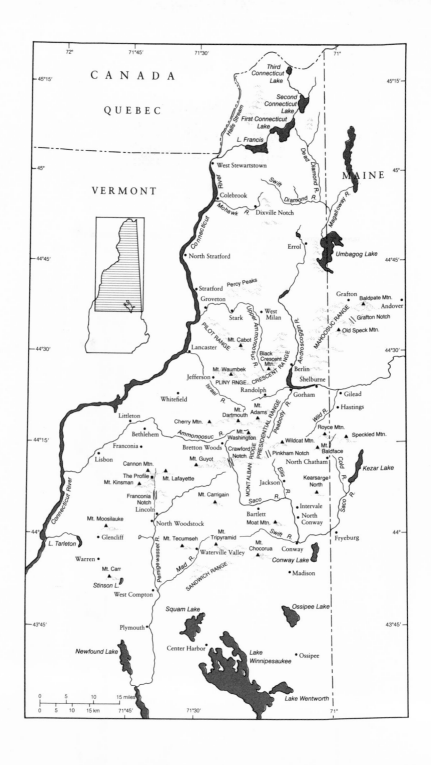

PLACE NAMES
of the WHITE
MOUNTAINS

REVISED EDITION

Robert and Mary Julyan

University Press of New England

HANOVER AND LONDON

With love and hope

we dedicate this book to our daughter,

MEGAN MAE JULYAN

University Press of New England, Hanover, NH 03755
© 1993 by Robert and Mary Julyan
Printed in the United States of America   5   4   3   2   1
CIP data appear at the end of the book
Designed by James F. Brisson

CONTENTS

ACKNOWLEDGMENTS

Preparation of a book such as this clearly would have been impossible   vii
without the kind cooperation of many persons, and to them we are
sincerely grateful. For the first edition of this book, we owe a special
debt of gratitude to the entire staff of Weeks Memorial Library in
Lancaster for their assistance, patience, and trust. Also deserving of
special appreciation are Bill and Iris Baird of Lancaster; Joe and Virginia Richardson of Lancaster; Edna Whyte of Lancaster; Glenn J.
Ackroyd of Gorham; Elaine D. Adjutant of Ossipee; Barbara Berry
of Wolfeboro Falls; Samuel I. Bowditch of Tucson, Arizona, and Chocorua; George E. Brixton of Wolfeboro; Marjorie E. Broad of Campton; Mrs. C. L. Dodge of Lisbon; Alfred L. Dowden of Ossipee;
Donald A. Lapham of Wolfeboro; James Mykland of Center Sandwich; Richard Roberts of Woodstock, Connecticut; Chilton Thom-
son of Cleveland, Ohio; and Frederic L. Steele of the White Mountain
School in Littleton. We are also grateful to Peter E. Randall and Walter Wright for their assistance with the original manuscript.

But since the book was originally published in 1980, and during
our revision, we have become indebted to numerous other persons
for their knowledge and goodwill. These persons include: Wilbur
Willey, historian, Littleton Area Historical Society; Roger Payne,
Chief, Branch of Geographic Names, Domestic Geographic Names,
U.S. Geological Survey; and Rebecca E. Oreskes and other personnel
with the White Mountains National Forest. We are especially grateful
to Douglass P. Teschner, without whose encouragement this present
book likely would not have happened.

April 1993   R. and M. J.

HOW TO USE THIS BOOK

This book contains approximately 650 names, listed alphabetically according to their specific term, not their generic (or their directional, or their indicator of size). Thus Mount Washington is under Washington, Mount; South Carter is under Carter, South; Big Attitash is under Attitash. This book also contains extensive cross-referencing. Where there have been name changes, previous names are cross-referenced to the present name; names with variants are cross-referenced to the most commonly accepted variant (if one exists); and if any confusion exists as to what name is current or what variant is accepted, we have chosen the form approved by the U.S. Board on Geographic Names (USBGN), as listed in the U.S. Geological Survey Geographic Names Information System (GNIS) Phase I inventory. Italicized place names in the text indicate that an entry will be found for it elsewhere.

We have not included guides to pronunciation, except where the locally accepted pronunciation is different from what a speaker of standard English would expect. Thus we have noted that Berlin locally is pronounced BURR-lin and not like the city in Germany.

We've attempted to list the elevation for each mountain, taking this from the GNIS, or where not given there, from U.S. Geological Survey (USGS), White Mountains National Forest (WMNF), and Appalachian Mountain Club (AMC) maps, noting which elevations are approximations.

Because of the great size of the White Mountains region, and because many place names are duplicated within it, we have listed opposite each name the subregion in which the feature is located (and have alphabetical duplicate entries by subregion). The designation of subregions has been *very* difficult, and often we've been reminded of H. L. Mencken's dictum that for every complex problem there's a simple solution—that doesn't work. River basins overlap mountain ranges, and both usually are ignored by political delineations. We finally chose to follow the system of regional subdivisions used by the AMC in its guidebooks. For example, if we have listed a name as being in the Carter-Moriah Range, the place it designates is located in the Carter-Moriah Range section of the AMC guide, 25th edition. The only exception to this is along the Connecticut River, where we have included names from areas not covered by the AMC guide. For this we have created a special subregion called the Connecticut Region.

We also tried to indicate within each entry's text where the feature was located relative to major landmarks. But, while we have tried assiduously to make the locations as accurate and current as possible, this book is a guide to names, not locations, and is not intended as a substitute for a good map.

The U.S. Board on Geographic Names (USBGN)

Imagine the chaos if individuals had one name on their driver's license, another on their banking records, another on their medical records, and still others on other documents. Last century, when vast new areas of the U.S. were being explored and mapped, the confusion of names on government maps and publications was similar to the above situation, so much so that in 1890 the U.S. Board on Geographic Names was created to standardize names appearing on federal maps, such as those created by the U.S. Geological Survey and the U.S. Forest Service. Since then the USBGN has continued to set policy and make decisions regarding new names and name changes. The primary criterion for most USBGN decisions is local usage. The USBGN publishes its decisions regularly, and decisions regarding White Mountains names have been incorporated into this book.

Disputes regarding place names have been common in the White Mountains. The most famous example is the name of the mountain east of Conway now known as Kearsarge North. We have encountered many such conflicts in preparing this book. Where two or more names exist in common usage, as with Mount Clinton-Pierce, we have made our primary entry the form approved by the USBGN as listed in the Geographic Names Information System, using cross-references for variant names.

The Geographic Names Information System (GNIS)

Beginning around 1960, the USGS recognized a growing need for a relatively complete inventory of the nation's three to five million place names, and by 1978 burgeoning computer technology had made such an inventory possible. Undertaken with the cooperation and support of the USBGN, the GNIS consists of a two-phase state-by-state inventory of the nation's place names. Phase I consisted of inventorying all names appearing on USGS quadrangles, the basic large-scale maps of the U.S. Phase II, which has not been completed for New Hampshire or Maine, will add to the original database many more names and much more information, gleaned from other federal, state, and local maps, as well as from historic maps, charts, postal records, census records, county histories, oral traditions, and other sources. Phase II will also research and record name variants.

While neither Phase I nor Phase II includes detailed historical or anecdotal information about names, GNIS nonetheless contributes greatly to a more detailed and accurate portrait of a state's namescape, and it has been a great asset in the preparation of this book, allowing us to record the distribution of certain common names, as well as to ascertain their locations. Also, because the GNIS names are, by definition, those accepted by the USBGN and thus the only ones that may be used on federal maps, such as WMNF and USGS maps, we have in the case of variants used as our primary entry the form approved by GNIS, noting other variants in the text and cross-references. Knowledgeable local people may challenge the GNIS form of a name, and if they feel strongly enough they may propose changing the GNIS name through the USBGN.

The Indians of the White Mountains

Readers of this book possibly will be confused by numerous references to Indian groups. Sokosis, Pequakets, Penacooks, Coösaukes—all are mentioned as having lived in the White Mountains, and the relationships among these groups often appear ill-defined. This confusion in part results from the fact that white settlers and explorers who wrote about these groups were not always clear about Indian identities; very often the name of an Indian village would be mistaken for a tribal name, as seems to have happened with Penacook, the name of a village near Concord. Also, Indian demography often was indeed complex.

To simplify matters, remember that all the groups mentioned as living in the White Mountains were Abenakis, a group of linguistically related tribes located along the major rivers of Maine, New Hampshire, Vermont, and adjacent areas of Massachusetts and Quebec. They called themselves Wabanaki, meaning "dawn land people," or "eastern people," and their language was part of the larger Algonquian group.

The Abenakis had two main divisions. The Eastern Abenakis lived for the most part in Maine, though one subdivision, the Pigwacket (or Pequawket), lived along the Saco River and inhabited the region around Conway and certainly traveled elsewhere in the White Mountains.

Most of the Indians in the White Mountains belonged to the Western Abenaki group, whose subdivisions included the Sokosis (or Sokoki), Pennacook, Winnipesaukee, and Coösauke (or Cowasuck).

Both groups became embroiled in the colonial conflicts between the French and the English and between the English and themselves, and during the French and Indian Wars the Abenakis were allies of the French. Both the eastern and western groups gradually fled northward to Quebec, where, except for the Penobscots in Maine, they live today; they numbered about 1,000 in the late 1970s, with about 250 at Saint Francis village at Odanak. A few Abenakis still speak the Eastern and Western Abenaki dialects.

Folk-Etymology and Indian Names

Ask someone about the popular Randolph trailhead labeled Appalachia, and you're likely to hear a story about how some boys overindulged on green apples here, inspiring local wags to name the site *Apple-ache-ia.* It is an appealing story, but it almost certainly owes more to ingenuity than to reality. More likely, the railroad that built the station preceding the trailhead named it for the Appalachian Mountains.

Appalachia is an excellent example of the process, well known to scholars of names, wherein people invent, not always consciously, a plausible explanation for a name whose real origin they don't know. The process is called *folk-etymology,* and examples in the White Mountains are numerous. How often, for example, is it repeated that Pilot Mountain on the Kilkenny Ridge was named for the little dog of an eccentric recluse who lived on the mountain? Yet the history of that name makes clear that the name existed before the recluse and resulted from the mountain's being a landmark, acting like a "pilot." At least three stories—all apocryphal—have evolved to explain the name of Tumbledown-Dick, a mountain in the Mahoosuc Range.

This is not to debunk names having colorful origins, as many names indeed do, but rather to encourage a healthy skepticism regarding some of the explanations common in the White Mountains—

and especially those having to do with Indians and so-called legends involving them.

Indians did name places in the White Mountains; indeed, Indians characteristically create a very high density of names in the places they inhabit. But, regrettably, few of these names have survived. Those that have remained tend to be in keeping with Indian names elsewhere in North America: the names simply describe the place. Ammonoosuc, "fish place," Coös, "pines," Androscoggin, "fish-curing place," Umbagog, "clear lake."

Furthermore, there's no reason to believe the Indians of the White Mountains differed from their fellows elsewhere in regarding as completely alien the concept of naming places to honor individual people. Thus the Indians' names in the White Mountains—Weetamoo, Passaconaway, Metallak, Kancamagus, and many more—were given by non-Indians, often a century or more after the individuals had lived, many during the nineteenth century, a time when romanticism regarding Indians greatly distorted reality.

And finally, we should be aware that the written forms of Indian names likely bear little resemblance to how the Indians actually would have pronounced them. Many early settlers could barely write English, much less accurately transliterate Indian words whose sounds and forms were completely alien. Written records contain at least fifty variant spellings of the name Winnipesaukee.

It's unfortunate more Indian names haven't survived, and we should be grateful for those that have. But as with folk-etymology, a healthy skepticism is appropriate for all Indian names and legends.

INTRODUCTION

This book is about the names, the places, and ultimately the people of the White Mountains. Defined broadly, the region is vast. Beginning north of Lake Winnipesaukee and running north over a hundred miles to the Canadian border, it includes virtually the entire northern third of New Hampshire and portions of Maine on the east. The region encompasses not only the White Mountains and its many subranges, as well as isolated summits, but also the headwaters and drainages of several major rivers—the Connecticut, the Androscoggin, the Ammonoosuc, the Saco, and the Cold.

In any study of a region's place names, the places come first, the region's topography a tablet upon which many peoples have written. In the White Mountains, literally thousands of places exist, ranging in size and significance from major mountain groups to isolated boulders, from rivers to tiny rivulets. And most of these places have names, because a name is not an insignificant or irrelevant appendage but rather an integral part of a place's identity. As the American names scholar Kelsie Harder has observed, "a place without a name in one sense isn't really a place."

We have been forced to be somewhat arbitrary in selecting which names to include among the thousands existing in the White Mountains. Clearly, the names of major geographic features were to be included, even where their origins and meanings are obscure, as with Kearsarge North, or obvious and self-explanatory, as with Twin Mountain. We have sought to have an entry for each major named peak and for each of the major watercourses. We also have attempted to have an entry for each of the more important geopolitical features, such as towns and villages.

But this book is about names as much as it is about places. And some names are included simply because they pique curiosity, or carry with them an interesting story, or reveal something about the region's history, even though the place itself has little significance or general recognition. Chickwolnepy Brook in the Mahoosuc Range, for example, has little to distinguish it—except its name. And in the town of Lancaster is a rural district similar to many others in the area except that it is known as Lost Nation—yet who could resist curiosity about this name?

And, ultimately, this book is about the people of the White Mountains, for they gave the names. Place names, paradoxically, are at the same time the most enduring and the most ephemeral of human cultural artifacts. Of the Indian peoples who inhabited the White Mountains for thousands of years, little has survived in our general consciousness—except a few of their names. Yet the Indian names that have not survived have vanished utterly, forever beyond recall.

Place names also are extraordinarily revealing of human culture; study a region's names and you will gain insight into the lives, the languages, and the values of the people that lived and traveled in that region. In the White Mountains, names have been given by explorers, settlers, legislators, local officials, farmers, fishermen, hunters, organizations, scientists, soldiers, and storytellers. The names recall presidents, wandering tinkers, English noblemen, obscure settlers, famous statesmen, eccentric hermits, hikers, Indians, merchants, roadbuilders, innkeepers, poets, artists, and even mythical figures. Some names, such as Spruce Mountain, are prosaically descriptive; others, such as Dianas Baths, are poetically fanciful.

Indians were the first name-givers in the White Mountains. Of their history and culture here little remains. By 1800 most of them had vanished from the region, their numbers decimated by disease and warfare, their lands occupied by ever-increasing numbers of white settlers. Linguistic studies of the Abenaki-speaking survivors of these peoples have been undertaken by such scholars as Father Rales, Rev. John Aubrey, and Prof. John C. Huden, and their work provides valuable insights into how Indians created names in the White Mountains. Here, as with Indian names throughout North America, Indian place names tend to be overwhelmingly descriptive. The name Ammonoosuc means simply "fish-place"; the name Pemigewasset means "swift current." This is not to imply that Indian naming or Indian cultures are simple—very often religious or ceremonial names coexist with everyday names—but rather to state that Indians often view the function of names very differently from persons of European ancestry.

For example, Indians have very different concepts of honor and posterity. As the Indian anthropologist Alfonso Ortiz once put it: "Indians want to be remembered, not written about—they're different things." Many place names in the White Mountains honor Indian personages: Chocorua, Paugus, Metallak, Kancamagus, Weetamoo, and others. But these names *all* were assigned by whites, and usually long after the Indians they honored had departed. They are more the stuff of legend than of history (see Folk-Etymology and Indian Names).

Non-Indian naming in the White Mountains began not long after Europeans arrived in northeastern North America. The name Christall Hill, likely referring to Mount Washington, appeared as early as 1628, in the writing of the mariner Christopher Leavitt. The first European to climb Mount Washington was Darby Field, who made his ascent in 1642—130 years before the American Revolution. Field's motives for the ascent are obscure; perhaps he sought treasure, or a route northward, or simply the adventure of being the first to stand on the mountain's summit. In any event, Field reported that his party "found nothing worth their pains." But while Field made mountaineering history, he left no names that endured.

Indian danger and remoteness kept most whites out of the White Mountains for about a hundred years, until 1761, when Gov. Benning Wentworth, the first royal governor of New Hampshire, began making extensive land grants, often to veterans of the French and Indian Wars, so that settlers might develop the new territories. Gov. Benning Wentworth was succeeded in 1767 by his nephew, John Wentworth, who was governor until 1775, and together the Wentworth governors granted and named most of the towns in the White Mountains. Almost invariably the names they assigned honored the Wentworths' business and political associates in England. Many of these names subsequently were changed, especially when the lands they designated were not settled; other names survive, in towns such as Bath, Colebrook, Conway, Errol, Landaff, Northumberland, and Stewartstown. Many persons selected by the Wentworths to be so honored were influential Englishmen who advocated mild treatment of the American colonies.

When the Revolutionary War broke out, the Wentworths departed. When a new nation emerged from the conflict, so did a new era of naming in the White Mountains. Americans instead of Englishmen were honored. Mount Washington was named during this period, as were most of the other peaks of the Presidential Range. The town of Columbia on the upper Connecticut River received its name during the patriotic enthusiasm preceding the War of 1812. Signers of the Declaration of Independence were honored by place names in the White Mountains, as were other prominent figures of the Revolutionary era.

At the same time scientific expeditions, such as the one led by Dr. Jeremy Belknap (1744–1798), began entering the White Mountains, and many place names honor early scientists, mapmakers, and explorers: Manasseh Cutler, Philip Carrigain, Jacob Bigelow, Francis Boott, Lemuel Shaw, Edward Tuckerman, and others. Many early explorers were botanists; rarely has the exploration and naming of geographical features owed so much to the search for plants.

But throughout this period, while formal commemorative names were being bestowed, other less formal but no less important or enduring names were sprouting. Settlers of the White Mountains needed names to identify brooks, mountains, fords, clearings, trails, notches, and so forth. Very often the names were not assigned but just sprang up in common usage. A pond where a man named Ladd settled became known as Ladd Pond; a path following an open artificial waterway became the Aqueduct Path; a settlement that grew up around a sawmill built by a man named Kidder became Kidderville; the notch where Daniel Pinkham tried to build a road became Pinkham Notch; and the pond where a man named Diamond shot a moose took the name Diamond Pond.

Local people liked to talk about the place names in their vicinity, and legends and tall tales grew up around them. In this book we have frequently and unashamedly used phrases such as "according to tradition" and "legend says." There is no way of verifying whether these tales are true or not. Very often they are the only information that exists regarding a name. And, even when a legend likely is apocryphal, we have still included it, because such legends are part of the character and color of the place (see Folk-Etymology and Indian Names).

By the mid-1800s a new group of people were coming to the White Mountains—tourists—and increasingly hotels, railroads, and paths were built to accommodate them. These people included writers and artists, and they were as much interested in recreation and communion with nature as in scientific exploration and adventure. Nathaniel Hawthorne wrote his famous short story about the Old Man of the Mountain; Rev. Thomas Starr King popularized the region with his highly descriptive writings; Moses F. Sweetser and others produced popular guidebooks; landscape artists such as Benjamin Champney and Thomas Cole portrayed the mountains' rugged beauty; and men of letters such as Henry David Thoreau, Daniel Webster, and John Greenleaf Whittier visited the region. Products of the romantic and transcendentalist movements in American thought, their writings and the names they bestowed reflect the values current at the time. It was during this period that names such as Arethusa Falls, Dianas Baths,

Mount Avalon, and Cathedral Ledge, as well as names honoring Indian figures, appeared in the White Mountains.

The latter part of the nineteenth century was another important period of naming in the White Mountains, with two important events occurring in 1876. In that year N.H. state geologist Charles H. Hitchcock published his map of the White Mountains, and also in that year the Appalachian Mountain Club (AMC) was born.

Few persons have known as much about the White Mountains' history and geography as Charles H. Hitchcock. For forty years he was a professor of geology at Dartmouth College, and in 1868 he was appointed state geologist, in which role he undertook a geological survey of the state. He was a frequent and thorough traveler of the White Mountains, and many of its features were discovered by him and his associates. He also named many places, and literally dozens of names appear for the first time on the map he published in 1876.

On January 1, 1876, Prof. E. Charles Pickering mailed cards of invitation to fifty persons "interested in mountain exploration," and thus the AMC was conceived. The club was formally organized soon thereafter, and during the years since then the AMC has had a continuing, intimate, and constructive relationship with the White Mountains. Committees were formed on trail construction and maintenance, and AMC officers and members such as J. Rayner Edmands, William G. Nowell, and others were largely responsible for the system of trails and huts presently existing in the White Mountains. These AMC members named many of the trails they built, and in return many trails and features were named for them.

The AMC also set up a Committee on Nomenclature to study mountain names and to arbitrate disputes. For example, this committee ruled that Mount Clinton, which had been renamed Mount Pierce by the New Hampshire legislature, should retain its original name on AMC maps (thus it remains to this day). And this committee voted against changing the name of a mountain in the town of Northumberland from Cape Horn to Mount Lyon, as had been proposed. Many decisions have since been ratified by time and usage; some are still contested.

The last great period of naming in the White Mountains began late in the nineteenth century and continues today. Until the late nineteenth century, most land in White Mountains towns was owned by individuals as modest farms; logging was limited and localized, but several events occurred then that dramatically changed this. In 1867 the state of New Hampshire sold 172,000 acres, to local landowners but also to land speculators. Soon after, major rail lines were completed around and through the White Mountains. Then, in the 1880s, the sulfite process for reducing wood to pulp was introduced. Suddenly, immense profits were to be made with large-scale logging in the White Mountains. Logging railroads—at least seventeen existed, not counting spur lines—and logging camps sprang up throughout the White Mountains, even in remote areas. Most of these were ephemeral, and relatively few names resulted from this activity.

But wasteful cutting practices resulting in vast areas of previously scenic wilderness suddenly being clearcut, along with attendant forest fires and devastating floods from denuded watersheds, prompted cries for protection and preservation. As early as 1881 the New Hampshire legislature appointed a temporary committee to study forest depletion. A permanent Forestry Commission was created in 1885. The broad-based Society for the Protection of New Hampshire Forests was created in 1901. And in 1911 the Weeks Act authorized the purchase of much of the land in the White Mountains and the creation of the White Mountains National Forest. This activity has resulted in numerous new names—of trails, of campgrounds and picnic areas, of wilderness areas, of state forests, of special management areas.

These, then, are the place names of the White Mountains. Like the mountains themselves, they are subject in their details to continuing change, yet in their general outlines they preserve an enduring record of the region's history. The names also are interesting and fun, and we sometimes like to imagine the people who have lived and traveled in the White Mountains, sitting around telling stories and recounting reminiscences from their experiences. We have enjoyed preparing this book; we hope you enjoy reading it.

The origins and meanings of some place names have eluded us; records and recollections regarding these names are either incomplete or nonexistent. The study of place names is a continuing search, and we hope readers who can supply information about *any* name in the White Mountains will contact us.

Robert and Mary Julyan
c/o University Press of New England
23 S. Main St.
Hanover, N.H. 03755-2048

PLACE NAMES
of the WHITE
MOUNTAINS

A–Z Trail

This trail crossing the Willey Range connects the Avalon and Zealand Trails, whence the name.

Abeniki, Lake; Mountain (2,231 feet)   *North Country*

The Abenaki Indians once inhabited most of northern New England, including the White Mountains, but their relations with the English often were turbulent, and during the French and Indian Wars they were allies of the French. They gradually retreated northward to Quebec, where except for the Penobscots in Maine they live today. The name Abenaki, also spelled Abeniki, Abnaki and Wabanaki, is how these Indians refer to themselves and means "dawn land people." The peak forming the north flank of *Dixville Notch,* as well as the lake immediately east, are reminders of these people's presence in the White Mountains.

Acteon Ridge   *Waterville Valley Region*

Running from Bald Knob to *Jennings Peak,* this ridge recalls the twilight days of the *Pemigewasset* Indians. They had a village at Franklin, and it is said that their last sachem, or chief, was named Acteon. This ridge was named for him by Prof. C. E. Fay of Tufts College.

Adams, Mount (5,798 feet)   *Northern Peaks, Great Gulf*

Mount Adams, second highest peak in New England, is actually three summits, all closely related. The highest summit, 5,798 feet, was christened Mount John Adams on July 31, 1820, by the Weeks-Brackett naming party from nearby Lancaster (see *Presidential Range*).

The northernmost of these three peaks also is named for a president, also named Adams and also named John. In 1857 Rev. Thomas Starr King named this 5,470-foot summit in honor of the nation's sixth president, John Quincy Adams, son of President Adams.

And finally, in 1876, some AMC members jokingly referred to the most westerly peak as Sam Adams—and the name stuck. Today this 5,585-foot summit honors the American pamphleteer and advocate of independence, Samuel Adams.

Adams Mountain (approx. 1,050 feet)
Speckled Mountain Region

The Adams family cleared land and operated a farm near this mountain east of North *Chatham*.

Agassiz, Mount (2,378 feet)
Cannon, Kinsman

Formerly known both as Peaked Mountain and as Pickett Hill, this peak south of *Bethlehem* was renamed in 1876 by New Hampshire state geologist Charles H. Hitchcock to honor Jean Louis Rudolph Agassiz (1807–73), the great Swiss explorer and naturalist who visited the White Mountains in 1846 and again in 1870. As a scientist, Agassiz is best known for his theory, propounded in 1837, that the landforms of Europe were formed by a great sheet of ice, not the biblical Deluge. His visits to the White Mountains brought him corroborating evidence for his views.

Agassiz Basin
Pemigewasset-Carrigain

See *Indian Leap*.

Air Line Trail
Northern Peaks, Great Gulf

Eugene B. Cook and Laban M. Watson in 1882 cut this path leading from what is now the *Appalachia Trailhead* on U.S. Route 2 to *Mount Adams,* and its name probably is derived from their decision to follow a ridge line. All previous trails had followed valleys.

Akers Pond
North Country

This pond northwest of the village of *Errol* was named for the Akers family, who once owned much of the shoreline.

Albany *Chocorua, East Sandwich*

West of Conway is the town of Albany, whose boundaries include the peaks of *Chocorua, Paugus, Three Sisters, Pequawket,* and South *Moat.* Albany originally was chartered as Burton in 1766, most likely in honor of Gen. Jonathan Burton of Wilton, but in 1833 it was renamed Albany. Sources suggest the change occurred because the railroad from New York City to Albany, New York, was chartered in 1833.

Alpine Garden *Mount Washington, Southern Ridges*

It is not known exactly when or by whom this meadow between the *Tuckerman Ravine* Trail and the *Mount Washington* Auto Road was named, but it was called the Alpine Garden by Moses F. Sweetser in his 1876 White Mountains guide. The reason for the name is clear: the meadow, in proper season, is dappled with alpine wildflowers blooming as in a garden. Some of the diminutive arctic plants growing in the tundra here are found nowhere else in New England, and Alpine Garden has been designated a Research Natural Area by the WMNF.

Ames Mountain (2,270 feet) *Speckled Mountain Region*

Fisher Ames (1756–1808) was an American statesman, and from him comes the name of this peak near *Chatham.* Ames's cousin, Dr. Joshua Fisher, participated in Dr. Jeremy Belknap's expedition to the White Mountains in 1784.

Ammonoosuc (general)

Three rivers in the White Mountains—the *Upper Ammonoosuc,* the *Ammonoosuc* further south, and the *Wild Ammonoosuc* further south still—all derive their names from an Abenaki Indian word meaning "fish-place." The Abenaki root word is variously cited as "namaos-auke," "ompompanusuck," and "namaos-coo-auke," all having roughly the same meaning. "Namos" means "fish," and "-auke" is a suffix meaning "place." Thus, the names of the Ammonoosuc rivers in the White Mountains and the Amoskeag River in central New Hampshire have a common origin.

Ammonoosuc Lake *Franconia, Twin, Willey Ranges*

Tiny lake at the north end of *Crawford Notch,* named because its waters drain into the *Ammonoosuc River.*

Ammonoosuc Ravine · *Mount Washington, Southern Ridges*

One of the most direct routes to the upper slopes of the *Presidential Range* is up this steep ravine connecting the *Cog Railway* Base Station with *Lakes of the Clouds*. Its name is thought to have originated with Moses F. Sweetser, who named the ravine for the river that flows through it. Lucy Crawford in her diary tells the story of two travelers from Boston who in 1823 named the ravine "Escape Glen." As they made their way down it from Lakes of the Clouds, one of them nearly perished when a stump to which he was clinging broke off and he fell fifty feet. The biologist William Oakes (see *Oakes Gulf*) also made a hasty descent down what he called "the most villainous break-neck route." The Ammonsoosuc Ravine Trail was opened by the AMC in 1915, to allow hikers on the *Crawford Path* and visitors at the Lakes of the Clouds Hut a fast escape route during bad weather.

Ammonoosuc River · *Mount Washington, Southern Ridges*

The Ammonoosuc River, one of the major drainages of the White Mountains, heads at *Lakes of the Clouds,* flows through *Ammonoosuc Ravine,* then west through the Ammonoosuc River Valley to join the Connecticut River at Woodsville. The river's name, meaning in Abenaki "fish place"—see *Ammonoosuc (general)*—is appropriate; Ethan Allen Crawford is said to have taken 600 to 700 pounds of trout and salmon from this river annually.

Anderson, Mount (3,722 feet) · *Carrigain, Moat Regions*

Located northeast of *Carrigain Notch,* this peak was named by New Hampshire state geologist Charles H. Hitchcock in 1876 for John E. Anderson of Portland, Maine. Anderson was chief engineer of the Portland and Ogdensburg Railroad, which in 1875 had opened a line through *Crawford Notch.*

Androscoggin River · *Mahoosuc Range Area*

This name is derived from an Abenaki word meaning "fish-curing place." The Indians are reported to have called this river Amariscoggin, which has the same meaning.

Appalachia · *Northern Peaks, Great Gulf*

An important trailhead on U.S. Route 2 in Randolph, Appalachia received its name when it was a Boston and Maine Railroad station

(1896–1941). The station was intended primarily for guests of the Ravine House, but it also served as a meeting place for hikers. According to apocryphal tradition, the name was born one Sunday afternoon soon after the station was opened, when some boys on a Sunday school picnic from *Berlin* stole some green apples from the trees at the Ravine House. That night the boys sat in the station holding their stomachs in pain as they awaited transportation home. The sight so amused the guests of the Ravine House that, acting in committee, they unanimously approved naming the new train station "Apple-ache-ia." It was only natural that in time this would be elided to become Appalachia. It is an appealing story, but more likely the station was named for the *Appalachian Mountains.*

Appalachian Mountains

The name of one of North America's great mountain ranges, stretching from Georgia to Maine, originated at a poor Indian village in Florida. When the Spanish explorer Narvaez launched an expedition into Florida seeking cities of gold, he found instead only a very ordinary Indian village called Apalchen. The Spaniards remembered this name, and eventually it was used on maps to designate the vague and mountainous interior. Still later, changed in spelling and pronunciation to Appalachian, it came to refer to the mountains themselves.

At first this name was not applied to the entire mountain chain, however. Indeed, it was not until the nineteenth century that the huge system had a single name. Early settlers, like the Indians, had a limited, localized perspective and thus had difficulty recognizing the mountains as a single geographical unit; rather, they came to know parts of the Appalachians under several different names. Slowly, as awareness grew of the unity of the range, most of the local names were dropped until at last only two names remained as rivals— Appalachian and Allegheny. The matter was settled in 1861 by the geographer Arnold Henry Guyot (see *Mount Guyot*) as he prepared to publish an important geological study of the mountains. As the names scholar George R. Stewart tells it: "He apparently hesitated between names. His map, prepared in advance, used Allegheny, but his final title was *On the Appalachian Mountain System*. The authority of his study apparently established scientific usage, which filtered down through school geographies and eventually became popular usage also."

Appalachian Trail

Taking its name from the mountain chain it traverses, the Appalachian Trail stretches 2,135 miles from Springer Mountain in Georgia to Mount Katahdin in Maine. It was built by volunteers between 1922 and 1937 and is maintained by groups and individuals coordinated by the Appalachian Trail Conference. In 1968, with the National Trails System Act, this trail was designated the Appalachian National Scenic Trail, the nation's first.

Appleby Brook, Mountain (2,321 feet) *North Country*

These features east of *Cherry Mountain* are said to take their name from Zebedee Applebee, an early settler.

Aqueduct Path *Carter, Baldface Ranges*

At one time this path, linking N.H. Route 16 with Nineteenmile Brook Trail, followed an open artificial waterway to the *Glen House*. This trail now is closed to hiking.

Arethusa Falls *Franconia, Twin, Willey Ranges*

Perhaps the highest single waterfall in the White Mountains, this cascade on *Bemis Brook* was discovered in 1840 by Prof. Edward Tuckerman. In his 1887 *Handbook for Travelers* Moses F. Sweetser wrote that the falls had been largely ignored subsequently "and are well nigh forgotten. They were visited and measured by the Editor and Professor Huntington in September, 1875, and then (being nameless) received the provisional name of Arethusa Falls, in allusion to Shelley's lines." Sweetser was referring to the poem written in 1820 by the English poet Percy Bysshe Shelley about a Greek myth of a water nymph named Arethusa, who, attempting to flee the advances of the river god, Alpheus, was transformed into a fountain. Rev. Thomas Starr King quoted this poem in his popular 1859 book, *The White Hills*.

Artist Brook, Falls *Carter, Baldface Ranges*

Benjamin Champney (1817–1907) was a nineteenth-century landscape painter who deeply loved the White Mountains, and he and several other landscape painters made the mountains, glens, streams, and waterfalls of the region their special province. They were particularly attracted to this brook between Mounts Cranmore and Peaked, and they spent many days painting along it. *Champney Brook* and *Champney Falls* on *Mount Chocorua* also recall the memory of this pioneer White Mountains artist. But, according to Bruce and Doreen Bolnick, in their *Waterfalls of the White Mountains,* these falls are more impressive in art than in reality. As the Bolnicks explain: "Despite its fetching name, this was never much of a spectacle. Artist Falls was a favorite subject for painters who preferred a short walk to a teensy waterfall over a long walk to something worthwhile. Evidently it is easier to embellish a painting than to tote art supplies over mountain trails."

Artists Bluff (2,340 feet) *Cannon, Kinsman*

This small summit northeast of *Cannon Mountain* bears on its southeast face a scenic cliff, for which the mountain was named.

Atkinson, Mount (940 feet) *Carter, Baldface Ranges*

At the south end of *Conway Lake* is this mountain named for Theodore Atkinson (1697–1779), secretary of state under the Wentworth governors (he married Benning Wentworth's sister) and a landowner in the town of *Jefferson.* The town of Atkinson is also named for him. The name Mount Atkinson appeared on Samuel Holland's map of 1784.

Atkinson and Gilmanton Academy Grant *North Country*

Two important eductional institutions in colonial New Hampshire gave their names to this 13,000-acre expanse of timberland in northern New Hampshire next to the Maine border. These lands were granted to the two academies in 1809 to hold in equal shares, from which they were to derive income. The academies were named for two then-prominent Federalist families.

Attitash Mountain *Carrigain, Moat Regions*

In his White Mountains guide, Moses F. Sweetser named Attitash Mountain for the Indian name for blueberries, which grew profusely on the mountain's slopes. Big Attitash Mountain, 2,936 feet, has been called West Moat on some maps (see *Moat Mountain*), but Big Attitash Mountain is the name accepted by the USBGN, and now the term West Moat is applied to the ridge connecting Big Attitash Mountain with North Moat. Little Attitash Mountain, 2,518 feet, approximately 1.5 miles northeast of Big Attitash Mountain, is now the site of a ski area.

Austin Mill Brook *Mahoosuc Range Area*

Heading at *Gentian Pond* and flowing south into the *Androscoggin River,* this brook probably takes its name from the family name of Hope Austin, who in 1781 settled in *Shelburne* with his wife and three children. It has appeared on some maps simply as Austin Brook.

Avalanche Brook *Waterville Valley Region*

In 1869 and 1885 great avalanches roared down *Mount Tripyramid,* giving this brook on the mountain's northwest slopes its name.

Avalanche Brook *Mount Washington, Southern Ridges*

Originally called Cow Brook, this stream on *Mount Webster* was renamed Avalanche Brook by Rev. Starr King, because the brook flows near the site of the fatal landslide in *Crawford Notch* that in 1826 wiped out the Willey family (see *Mount Willey*). Cow Brook, felt the poetic King, was too mundane a name for such a tragic site.

Avalanche Falls *Franconia, Twin, Willey Ranges*

This cascade at the head of the Flume on Flume Brook was once called Flume Cascade, but the current name, whose specific origin is unknown, avoids confusion with the better known Flume below.

Avalon, Mount (3,432 feet) *North Country*

Moses F. Sweetser thought this spur of *Mount Field* resembled the hills of Avalon on the Newfoundland peninsula. In Britain Avalon was King Arthur's legendary residence and burial place.

Aziscoös Lake *North Country*

The name of this North Country lake straddling the Maine-New Hampshire border is Abenaki for "small pine trees."

Bad Mountain (approx. 1,250 feet)

Speckled Mountain Region

Topographic maps show relatively gentle slopes here, challenging the explanation that the name of this small mountain north of *Miles Notch* resulted from the mountain being difficult to climb, and giving credence to the explanation that a family named Bad lived here.

Baker River   *Moosilauke Region*

Where the Baker River joins the *Pemigewasset River* was once an Indian resort area. In 1712, during the Indian wars, Indians engaged in games here were attacked by a party of whites from Haverhill, Massachusetts, led by Capt. Thomas Baker. Many Indians were killed in the battle, much fur was destroyed, and the victor's name was given to the river where the battle occurred. Another account of the incident says most of the camp's men were away at the time of the attack; old men, women, and children were the primary casualties. When the warriors returned and pursued the raiders, Captain Baker built numerous campfires, leading the Indians to believe the white party was much larger than it was, and the Indians abandoned the chase. Captain Baker's attitudes toward Indians had been colored by his capture in 1804 during the Deerfield raid; on the forced march to Canada he'd seen many of his fellow captives killed when they lagged behind. Later, Captain Baker escaped and returned to Massachusetts. The Indian name for the river is said to have been Asquamchumauke, which has been translated from Abenaki as "salmon spawning place" and also as "water of the mountain place."

Bald (general)

Wherever a mountain's summit is naked of trees—through fire, elevation, or other circumstances—people frequently call it "bald," a name repeated in various forms on barren summits throughout the world. In the White Mountains, more than fifteen features have *bald* in their names.

Bald Cap (3,065 feet)   *Mahoosuc Range Area*

Bald Cap Peak (2,795 feet)

Bald Cap, North (2,893 feet)

Three summits related by location and name (see *Bald [general]*). They are said to have been named by Eugene B. Cook and his family. Some guides refer to Bald Cap Peak as Bald Cap Dome.

Baldface, North (3,591 feet)   *Carter, Baldface Ranges*

Baldface, South (3,569 feet)

Baldface Range

The Baldface Range northwest of North *Chatham* is a treeless ridge—whence the name—whose principal summits are North Baldface and South Baldface. Baldface Knob, approx. 2,990 feet, is a prominence on the southeast shoulder of South Baldface.

Baldpate, Mount (3,812 feet)   *Mahoosuc Range Area*

The second highest of the peaks near the Maine-New Hampshire border, this mountain is sometimes known as Bear River Whitecap and also as Saddleback. Baldpate is a common descriptive metaphor for a treeless summit.

Barnes Field Campground   *Northern Peaks, Great Gulf*

This site near the *Dolly Copp Campground* was where the Barnes family farmed in the mid-1800s.

Bartlett   *Carrigain, Moat Regions*

Dr. Josiah Bartlett (1729–95) of Kingston, a physician whose signature appears just beneath that of John Hancock on the Declaration of Independence, was honored in 1790 by having this town named for him. Dr. Bartlett also became New Hampshire's first "governor," his predecessors having been called "presidents." The town originally had been granted in the 1760s to four officers of the French and Indian Wars, but they never claimed their land so it was regranted later.

Bartlett, Mount (2,661 feet) *Carter, Baldface Ranges*

Like the town, this mountain east of *Intervale* was named for Dr. Josiah Bartlett (see *Bartlett*).

Bartlett Haystack (2,995 feet) *Carrigain, Moat Regions*

This descriptively named summit southwest of *Bartlett*, east of *Sawyer Pond*, previously had been called Mount Silver Spring, in a time when, as the AMC Guide puts it, "Hazy elegance was preferred to plain and effective description." The peak also has been called Revelation, for reasons unknown.

Bath *Connecticut Region*

The town of Bath, between *Woodsville* and *Lisbon*, was named in 1761 for the prominent English statesman William Pulteney (1684–1764), first Earl of Bath and a brilliant scholar and orator. Poultney, Vermont, once part of New Hampshire, also was named for him.

Bean Brook *North Country*

Bean Brook is the first stream above *Berlin Falls* on the *Androscoggin River,* and it crosses what once was the farm of Benjamin Bean, an early settler in the town of *Success.*

Beans Grant *Mount Washington, Southern Ridges*

In 1831 an act of the New Hampshire legislature authorized the governor to sell previously unassigned public lands, and in 1835 this 3,300-acre mountain tract above *Crawford Notch* was granted to Charles Bean of Maine. Beans Grant, now in the WMNF, includes *Mount Jackson,* 4,052 feet, and *Mount Eisenhower,* 4,775 feet.

Beans Purchase *Carter, Baldface Ranges*

In 1832 Alpheus Bean of *Bartlett* purchased this 33,000-acre wilderness tract, stretching east from *Pinkham Notch* to the Maine border, for $1,033. It was one of the largest grants made by land commissioner James Willey in the 1830s, and it included *Mount Moriah,* the *Carter* Range, and *Wildcat Mountain.* Beans Purchase is now entirely within the WMNF.

Bear Mountain (3,217 feet)   *Carrigain, Moat Regions*

Names such as this often are thought to result from an abundance of bears in the area, but more likely the name resulted from a long-forgotten incident involving a bear. Bear Notch, sometimes called Bear Mountain Notch, separates Bear Mountain on the southeast and Mount Silver Spring (*Bartlett Haystack*) on the northwest; and during the nineteenth century it was traversed by a railroad line transporting lumber.

Bear Mountain (approx. 3,100 feet)   *Mahoosuc Range Area*

The specific origin of this name has been forgotten. This sprawling mountain has several summits, the southern one being Campbell Mountain, approx. 2,880 feet. Further south along the ridge is Little Bear Mountain, approx. 1,860 feet.

Beaver (general)

The earliest European explorers in North America often were trappers, and they especially were eager to locate beavers. Thus Beaver names are common on water bodies throughout North America. GNIS lists seventeen Beaver Brooks in New Hampshire, seven Beaver Ponds, as well as Beaver Lake, Beaver Meadow Brook, Beaver Dam Pond, Beaverdam Brook, and Beaver Wood Pond. Beaver Brook Cascades, west of North Woodstock, are among the most scenic in the White Mountains. Also noteworthy are Beaver Brook Falls, northeast of Colebrook.

Beckytown   *Waterville Valley Region*

In Waterville Valley a woman named Rebekah Blanchard once lived with her husband in the deep woods. From time to time she would get lonesome, so she would walk two miles to the edge of a pasture overlooking a settlement. There, too shy to visit, she would tarry and gaze at the activity below. Local residents became aware of her presence and came to call the clearing where she lived Beckytown.

Beecher Cascade   *Franconia, Twin, Willey Ranges*

Rev. Henry Ward Beecher (1813–87) was a New York Congregationalist minister who became famous for his oratory and for his abolitionist crusades. After 1872 Reverend Beecher often spent summers in the White Mountains, often accompanied by his sister, Harriet Beecher Stowe, author of *Uncle Tom's Cabin*. This waterfall on Crawford Brook was named in his honor. Originally his name was on a series of waterfalls here, then called in the plural Beechers Cascades, but since then the fall and the name have become singular.

Bee Line Trail   *Chocorua, East Sandwich*

This trail is named because two of its sections make a "bee line" between the summits of *Mounts Chocorua* and *Paugus*.

Bemis Brook, Lake, Ridge; Mount (3,706 feet)
                    Carrigain, Moat Regions

Dr. Samuel Bemis was a Boston dentist who spent the summers of 1827–40 in *Harts Location*. An enthusiastic photographer, the area's beauty enchanted him. (He was among the first Americans to import a daguerrotype camera from Europe following its invention in 1839.) He built a fine stone house known as *Notchland* in *Crawford Notch*, where he resided full time until his death in 1881. The house, which also has served as an inn, still stands.

Dr. Bemis was called "the Lord of the Valley," and he has been described as "one of the most devoted and genial disciples Izaak Walton ever had." He was an enthusiastic explorer of the White Mountains, and the names of *Mount Crawford, Mount Resolution,* and *Giant Stairs* were suggested by him. In return for his interest, a mountain, a brook, a ridge, and the locality where he lived all were named for him.

Benton   *Moosilauke Region*

This town on the *Wild Ammonoosuc River* in southeastern *Grafton County* originally was named Coventry, but in 1839 Gov. Isaac Hill renamed it to honor his friend Thomas Hart Benton, U.S. Senator from Missouri, who favored westward expansion. In 1840 the town was incorporated under its new name.

Berlin

Massachusetts, not Germany, gave this industrial city in north-eastern New Hampshire its name, and the town's citizens pronounce the name with the accent on the first syllable—BURR-lin—rather than on the second, to distinguish it from the German city.

Actually, Berlin began its identity in 1771 as Maynesborough, a name suggested by Gov. John Wentworth to honor his friend and business associate, Sir William Mayne of London, who was associated with him in the extensive trade with the British West Indies colony of Barbados. Governor Wentworth also secured grants in the town for several other Barbados traders.

None of the Barbados grantees of Maynesborough, however, claimed their grants, and following the American Revolution the land gradually was settled by persons from the Worcester County, Massachusetts, towns of Lancaster, Bolton, and Berlin.

Berlin Falls

Now erased by a dam, these falls on the *Androscoggin River* inspired Rev. Thomas Starr King to write in 1868: "We do not think that in New England there is any passage of river passion that will compare."

Bethlehem

The name Bethlehem for this northern *Grafton County* town was conceived on Christmas Day in 1799, and the incorporation papers were signed on Dec. 27, 1799, by Gov. John T. Gilman. Earlier, since 1774, the town had been known as Lloyds Hills, which commemorated the granting in 1773 of 23,000 acres to James Lloyd of Boston.

Bickford Brook

By 1787 Benjamin Bickford had settled in this part of Maine; this brook, heading on Ames Mountain and flowing southwest to join the *Cold River* north of North *Chatham*, takes its name from his family.

Big Attitash Mountain (2,936 feet) *Carrigain, Moat Regions*

See *Attitash Mountain.*

Bigelow Lawn *Mount Washington, Southern Ridges*

The White Mountains include several "lawns"—broad alpine meadows of tough arctic grasses and flowering plants left stranded by retreating glaciers. Bigelow Lawn on the southern shoulder of *Mount Washington* was appropriately named for Dr. Jacob Bigelow (1786–1879), a well-known New England botanist whose *Florula Bostoniensis* was the standard manual of New England botany until Gray's *Manual of Botany* appeared in 1848. In 1816 Dr. Bigelow led an exploratory party up Mount Washington (he referred to it as Mount Sugarloaf), seeking scientific knowledge. Bigelow Lawn was first noted on Bond's map of the White Mountains, published in 1853.

Black Cap (2,370 feet) *Carter, Baldface Ranges*

Conspicuous granite patches on its summit probably are responsible for the name of this peak in the *Green Hills* south of *Mount Kearsarge North*.

Black Crescent Mountain (3,265 feet) *North Country*

This summit at the northeast end of the *Crescent Range* originally had been called simply Mount Crescent, but that duplicated the name of another summit 2.75 miles southeast in the range, so in 1936 the USBGN approved the name Black Crescent Mountain, derived from the mountain's shape and hue.

Black Mountain 3,303 feet *Carter, Baldface Ranges*

Every state with mountains has several named Black Mountain—GNIS lists seven in New Hampshire—virtually all named for their dark appearance, often, as here, derived from swarthy vegetation such as conifers. This sprawling mountain north of *Jackson* has approximately seven summits, most unnamed. Best known is The Knoll, 1,910 feet, at the mountain's south end.

Blakes Pond *Connecticut Region*

Moses Blake and Walter Bloss were early settlers of the town of *Dalton* on the *Connecticut River*. This pond in the southeast corner of the township was named for Blake.

Blue, Mount (4,350 feet)   *Moosilauke Region*

Waternomee was the original name of this peak south of *Moosilauke Brook,* but it later is mentioned as Bog-eddy Mountain and as Mount Blue, the latter name having survived. It appeared as Mount Blue on Philip Carrigain's 1816 map of the White Mountains.

Blueberry Ledge   *Chocorua, East Sandwich*

Blueberry names are common in the Northeast, with GNIS listing eight in New Hampshire. The trail to this ledge on *Mount Whiteface* was opened in 1899.

Bolles Trail   *Chocorua, East Sandwich*

This trail between *Mounts Chocorua* and *Paugus* was named for Frank Bolles (1856–94), secretary of Harvard University and a Chocorua devotee. His chapter "Following a Lost Trail," in *At the North of Bearcamp Water,* Boston, 1893, describes its reexploration on Saturday, July 30, 1892.

Bond, Mount (4,698 feet)   *Franconia, Twin, Willey Ranges*
Bond, West (4,540 feet)
Bondcliff (4,265 feet)

These summits and associated cliffs south of *Mount Guyot* were named in 1876 by the AMC for Prof. G. P. Bond, the geographer who in 1853 made a comprehensive map of the White Mountains. West Bond is a spur of Mount Bond, while Bondcliff is approximately one mile south; this appears on some maps as simply The Cliffs.

Boott Spur (5,500 feet)   *Mount Washington, Southern Ridges*

It was over Boott Spur, the prominent ridge running south from *Mount Washington,* that many early ascents of the mountain were made. It is appropriate, therefore, that this ridge was named for Dr. Francis Boott, a physician and botanist who in 1816 was a member of Dr. Jacob Bigelow's scientific expedition to the White Mountains. Dr. Boott was the son of Kirk Boott, founder of Boott Mills at Lawrence, Massachusetts.

The Boott Spur Trail is regarded as the probable route Darby Field took during his ascent of Mount Washington in 1642. The ridge was called Davis's Spur on Bond's map of 1853, but by 1859 it was being called Boott Spur. The present Boott Spur Trail was laid out by the AMC in 1900.

Bowman, Mount (3,450 feet) *Northern Peaks, Great Gulf*

The origin of this name is in dispute, with two persons mentioned as possibly having given their names to this northwesterly spur of *Mount Jefferson.* The two were Jonas Bowman, an early settler of *Littleton* and tavernkeeper of *Kilkenny,* and the Hon. Selwyn Z. Bowman, who while a student acted as an assistant on a mountain survey in the White Mountains. Bowman also is the name of a locality on the Boston and Maine Railroad, between *Appalachia* and Highlands, at the north foot of Mount Bowman.

Boy Mountain (2,240 feet) *North Country*

Moses F. Sweetser in his White Mountains guide called this scenic viewpoint in *Jefferson* Boy Mountain. William Henry Pickering later wrote that he thought Ball Mountain was the knob's original name. It has appeared on maps under both names. Some people feel the present name is a corruption of Bois Mountain, which is derived from the French word for "wood."

Bragg Pond *North Country*

This pond in the town of *Errol* was named for the Bragg family, who cleared land and farmed here in the early days of settlement.

Bretton Woods *Franconia, Twin, Willey Ranges*

Now the name of a large and famous hotel-resort complex, Bretton Woods once was the name of the town of *Carroll,* where the resort is located. In 1772 the township of Bretton Woods was granted by Gov. John Wentworth to several persons, including his cousin, Sir Thomas Wentworth, who resided at Bretton Hall in Yorkshire, England. Bretton Hall was the ancestral home of the Wentworths.

The town was settled slowly, and in 1832 an act of the New Hampshire legislature changed the town's name to Carroll in honor of Charles Carroll of Carrollton, Maryland, and the name Bretton Woods fell into disuse for about seventy years until the resort was created.

Brickett Falls *Carter, Baldface Ranges*

These minor falls on Mill Brook west of North *Chatham* take their name from John Brickett, who arrived in the *Cold River* Valley in 1803, settling in a log cabin, clearing farmland, and growing corn and potatoes, as well as burning logs for potash. In 1812 he built a red-brick farmhouse, using bricks he fired himself; the well-preserved home still stands 0.5 miles east of the Cold River Campground. Bricketts resided in the farmhouse for generations, and their descendants still live in the area.

Bridal Veil Falls *Cannon, Kinsman*

In his *Heart of the White Mountains,* published in 1882, Samuel Adams Drake said this fall on *Coppermine Brook,* flowing down the western slope of *Cannon Mountain,* was named because of the "marvelous transparency, which permits the ledges to be seen through the gauze-like sheet falling over them."

Brook Path *Chocorua, East Sandwich*

Usually the origin of the name of a place is more interesting than the origin of the place itself. Not so for the Brook Path. This path up *Mount Chocorua* clearly was named because it follows Clay Bank Brook, but the path came into being as a way for country people to avoid paying tolls when going to gather blueberries on the upper slopes of Mount Chocorua. The other routes had tollgates on them under state charter.

Brunel Trail *Carrigain, Moat Regions*

Connecting the *Sawyer Pond* Trail with Mount Tremont, this trail was planned and blazed by Dr. Roger F. Brunel.

Bryce Path *Carrigain, Moat Regions*

This path to the summit of *Cathedral Ledge* was laid out in 1907 by British Ambassador James Bryce, hence the name. Bryce later became Viscount Bryce and the author of *The American Commonwealth,* an important study of American government from the British perspective.

The Bulge (3,920 feet)

Descriptively named summit on the south ridge of the *Pilot Range*, 0.5 miles northeast of *Mount Cabot.*

Bull Brook

Carter, Baldface Ranges

A logging team of bullocks somehow inspired the name of this brook, which heads on *East Royce Mountain* and flows north into *Evans Brook.*

Bumpus Basin, Brook

Northern Peaks, Great Gulf

Silas Bumpus was an early settler of *Randolph* and served as town clerk when the town was incorporated in 1824; these features between *Howker* and *Gordon Ridges* on *Mount Madison* are named for him.

Bungy

Cannon, Kinsman

Bungy, spelled in various ways, is a place name that occurs both near *Colebrook* and near *Sugar Hill.* The origin of the Colebrook name is unknown, but in Sugar Hill "Bungy-jar" is the south wind beginning to blow through *Kinsman* Notch; when the wind is high, people say "the Bungy Bull is a-blowing." It is said the wind invariably presages a storm, its high keening increasing in intensity until the storm actually arrives. The term is said to have originated when many early settlers, discovering that they could not farm successfully near Kinsman Notch, departed for better conditions. The remaining settlers said that those who had departed had "bunged-out."

Burnhams Brook

Franconia, Twin, Willey Ranges

This tributary of the *Ammonoosuc River* in the town of *Lisbon* was named for a hermit who built his cabin near its mouth. As civilization advanced, he left to seek a more secluded locality in the wilderness.

Burnt Knoll

Franconia, Twin, Willey Ranges

The most likely origin for this name is that it comes from the appearance of this knoll near *Mount Garfield* following great forest fires here in 1902. Guidebooks nearly twenty years later spoke of the "burned country."

Burt Ravine *Mount Washington, Southern Ridges*

Henry M. Burt was the founder and publisher of *Among the Clouds,* the daily newspaper established in 1877 atop the summit of *Mount Washington.* In 1901, the *Coös County* Commissioners named the ravine paralleling the Mount Washington Cog Railway to honor him.

Butters Mountain (2,246 feet) *Speckled Mountain Region*

The Butters family cleared land for a farm here, and thus gave their name to this mountain northeast of *Speckled Mountain.*

Butterwort Flume *Franconia, Twin, Willey Ranges*

Prof. J. D. Dana and Prof. Charles H. Hitchcock discovered this flume in 1875 while examining rocks on *Mount Willard* for the state geological survey. They named the ravine, most likely for the yellow butterwort flowers they found growing here.

C

Cabot, Mount (1,512 feet) *Mahoosuc Range*   21

On August 19, 1864, a group of guests at the Philbrook Farm Inn in *Shelburne* named this small mountain north of the *Androscoggin River* for Edward Cabot of Boston, a longtime guest at the inn.

Cabot, Mount (4,180 feet) *North Country*

Mount Cabot is the highest summit in the White Mountains north of the *Presidential Range*. It was named by the White Mountains explorer and enthusiast William Dandridge Peck for Sebastian Cabot (1476–1557), the sixteenth-century English pilot who explored the northeastern coast of North America.

Cambridge *North Country*

Cambridge, an unincorporated town south of *Errol,* took its name from Cambridge, Massachusetts, where Gov. John Wentworth graduated from Harvard in 1755. The charter was prepared in 1773 but apparently never issued.

Campton *Moosilauke Region*

Two conflicting explanations exist for the origin of the name of this town on the *Pemigewasset River.* The most widely accepted version is that the name came from early surveyors and settlers building their camp on the intervale beside the river. As the camp grew, the settlement took the name "Camptown"; this name appeared on the town's charter in 1761. With time Camptown became elided to Campton.

The other explanation is that Campton was named by Gov. Benning Wentworth to honor Spencer Compton, Earl of Wilmington, who was one of Wentworth's influential friends, so influential, in fact, that it was partly due to Compton's influence that Wentworth became governor in 1741. Governor Wentworth granted this town in 1761, and it was granted again in 1767, when the name was supposedly given. The difference between Compton and Campton is not necessarily significant, as spelling in the eighteenth century was less formalized than that of today, and the pronunciation of the vowel "a" was broader, as one might expect a Scotsman or an Irishman to speak it today. Thus Compton could easily have become Campton.

Cannon Mountain (4,077 feet)   *Cannon, Kinsman*

Many names have been applied to this peak, which forms the west flank of *Franconia Notch*. It appeared as Freak Mountain on Philip Carrigain's map of 1816 and as Old Mans Mountain on an 1852 map. Its other variants have included Frank Mountain, Old Man of the Mountain, and Jackson Peak. The mountain still is widely known as Profile Mountain, a name it bore as early as 1827 because on its east side is the famous profile known as *The Old Man of the Mountain.* The name Profile Mountain was promoted officially in 1927 following the successful effort by Rev. Guy Roberts of *Whitefield* to preserve the famous stone face. Apparently Roberts unearthed the old name while doing research during his campaign. But in 1972 the USBGN established Cannon Mountain as the accepted form. The name Cannon Mountain is derived from an oblong rock resting on a boulder near the summit that resembles a cannon when viewed from Profile Clearing. Three knobs on the *Kinsman* Ridge Trail, southwest of Cannon Mountain, are known as the Cannon Balls, with elevations east to west of 3,769 feet, 3,660 feet, and 3,693 feet.

Cape Horn (2,008 feet)   *North Country*

An odd squiggle of a mountain southeast of the village of *Groveton,* this formation is said by some local residents to be named for its resemblance when viewed from above to Cape Horn, South America. Others say it was named for its resemblance to a cow's horn, again when viewed from above. The mountain's outline corroborates both theories, though one wonders how often the early settlers viewed the mountain from above. An attempt was made in the last century to have the name changed to Lyon Mountain to honor a prominent railroad official, but the name was rejected by the AMC, and time has proved the club correct; the railroad official has been forgotten, but the name Cape Horn continues to intrigue people. The name Cape Horn appeared on Carrigain's 1816 map.

Caribou, Mount (2,828 feet)   *Speckled Mountain Region*

This mountain in the town of Mason, Maine, was called Calabo on the 1853 Walling map of Oxford County, Maine. The word "caribou" comes from the Algonquian Indian language, meaning "the pawer, the pawing animal"; the Micmac "kalibu" is close to the Walling name. The word "caribou" has passed into English via Canadian French. The mountain's present name doubtless was derived from the presence at one time of caribou in the vicinity, most likely the woodland variety, *Rangifer caribou*, exterminated long ago.

Caribou Speckled Wilderness Area
Speckled Mountain Region

This USFS wilderness area around *Evans Notch* was designated by the WMNF in 1991 and named for two prominent summits within its boundaries, *Mount Caribou* and *Speckled Mountain*.

Carlo, Mount (3,562 feet)   *Mahoosuc Range*

This peak was named for a dog at the Philbrook Farm Inn in *Shelburne*, a pet and companion of the well-known White Mountains hiker Eugene B. Cook.

Carmel, Mount (3,647 feet)   *North Country*

See *Rump Mountain*.

Carr, Mount (3,470 feet)   *Moosilauke Region*

Sometimes a place name preserves in perpetuity the memory of an otherwise insignificant incident; Mount Carr is an example. A man named Carr once wandered lost for two days in the mountains near the confluence of the *Pemigewasset* and *Baker Rivers* before he was finally rescued at *Warren*. The name Mount Carr appeared on Philip Carrigain's 1816 map.

Carrigain Brook, Notch, Pond; Mount (4,680 feet)

Carrigain, Moat Regions

Philip Carrigain was New Hampshire's secretary of state 1805–10, but he more often is remembered as a mapmaker. He surveyed much of the state, and in 1816 he published a map of New Hampshire that included many new names, such as *Mounts Stinson, Eastman, Willard,* and *Kinsman.* It is probably only fitting, therefore, that seven features in the White Mountains bear his name as well. (Perhaps inappropriately, a late eighteenth-century logging camp a mile south of *Bemis Brook* was named Carrigain.) Carrigain was a member of the Weeks-Brackett party of 1820 that named most of the *Presidential* peaks.

Carroll (town), County
Franconia, Twin, Willey Ranges

Wealth and patriotism made Charles Carroll of Maryland one of the best-known and respected men of revolutionary America. He was among the signers of the Declaration of Independence, and not only was his hometown, Carrollton, named for him but also a town and county in northern New Hampshire that history records he visited only once. In 1776, on assignment from Benjamin Franklin, Carroll made an unsuccessful journey to Montreal to discuss the possibility of a union between U.S. and French Canadian clergy, and he passed through the White Mountains wilderness en route. The town of Carroll was named for him in 1832, the year of his death; before that the town had been named *Bretton Woods.* Carroll County was named for him eight years later.

Carter Dome (4,843 feet)
Carter, Baldface Ranges
Carter, South (4,458 feet)
Carter, Middle 4,621 feet
Carter, North 4,539 feet

Carter Notch

As happened often in the White Mountains, an explorer interested in botany gave his name to geology. All the above major features, as well as Carter Ledge and Carter Boulders, were named for Dr. Ezra Carter, a Concord physician who in the early 1800s made frequent explorations in the White Mountains searching for medicinal herbs and roots. It also has been suggested, however, that the name might be derived from an early hunter. Moses F. Sweetser in his guide said legend told of two hunters, Carter and Hight, who traveled the mountains; see *Mount Hight*.

Cascade Brook   *Cannon, Kinsman*

Five waterfalls along this brook, including Kinsman Falls and Rocky Glen Cascades, named this stream that heads at *Lonesome Lake* and flows south and then southeast into the *Pemigewasset River* at *Franconia Notch*.

Cascade Brook, Ravine   *Northern Peaks, Great Gulf*

Cascade Ravine on the northwest shoulder of *Mount Adams* takes its name from six waterfalls along its course.

Cascade Brook   *Waterville Valley*

Heading in the *Sandwich Range* and flowing northwest to *Waterville Valley*, this stream takes its name from a series of waterfalls along it, reached by the Cascade Path.

Castellated Ridge   *Northern Peaks, Great Gulf*

Joining *Mount Jefferson* from the north, this ridge, also called Castle Ridge, was named for rock outcroppings along it known as Castles; see *Ridge of the Caps*. The Castle Trail ascending the ridge was cut in 1883–84 by Eugene B. Cook, Laban Watson, Albert Matthews, and Hubbard Hunt.

Cathedral Ledge   *Carrigain, Moat Regions*

Do you see a resemblance to a cathedral in a large cavity in the face of this cliff? Members of a family named Parsons, who visited North Conway prior to 1859, reportedly saw such a resemblance, and they gave the ledge its present name; before that it had been known as Harts Ledge. Beneath the cathedral cavity is another, known antithetically as *Devils Den*.

Cave Mountain (1,460 feet)
Mount Washington, Southern Ridges

This small summit just north of *Bartlett* was named for the cave in its south side.

Centennial Trail
Mahoosuc Range

In 1976 the AMC celebrated its 100th birthday, and in 1976 this trail ascending *Mount Hayes* was cut and named for the centennial.

Champney Brook Trail, Falls
Chocorua, East Sandwich

This route up *Mount Chocorua*, following Champney Brook and going past Champney Falls, was named for Benjamin Champney (1817–1907), an early landscape artist of the White Mountains who had his studio in North Conway from 1850. The trail was originally built by Prof. J. S. Pray and later cleared by the Chocorua Mountain Club. See *Artist Brook, Falls*.

Chandler Brook
Mahoosuc Range Area

It seems that any man owning a sawmill on this brook also possessed the right to have the brook named for him. Rising in the mountains east of the village of *Milan* and running through the town of *Success*, this brook is said to have once borne the Indian name "Nulliekunjewa," which is supposed to have meant "great fishing brook." It was later called Stearns Brook for Isaac Stearns, who built a sawmill on the brook about 1823, and still later it was called Paine Brook for Henry Paine, a subsequent owner of the mill. About 1850 Hazen Chandler and others bought the town of Success and built several larger mills on the brook, and Chandler's name has survived.

Chandler Brook
Mount Washington, Southern Ridges

Chandler Brook in the *Great Gulf* most likely recalls Jeremiah Chandler, for whom *Chandlers Purchase* was named.

Chandler Ridge
Mount Washington, Southern Ridges

On August 7, 1856, a 75-year-old hiker named Benjamin Chandler left for the summit of *Mount Washington*; he didn't return. A year later, on July 9, his body was found beneath a ledge under which he had apparently crawled for shelter and died. The northeast ridge of Mount Washington, where the ledge is located, was named for him.

Chandlers Purchase
Mount Washington, Southern Ridges

This narrow strip of land covering part of the western approaches to *Mount Washington,* including part of the Mount Washington *Cog*

Railway, was granted in 1835 to Jeremiah Chandler of *Conway* for $300.

Chatham   *Carter, Baldface Ranges*

William Pitt, Earl of Chatham and influential English statesman, had sympathy for the American colonists, arguing that England had no right to tax them and should adopt a "more gentle mode" of governing them. Today, the names of three New Hampshire towns honor him—Pittsfield, *Pittsburg,* and this scenic and sparsely populated town north of *Conway.*

Cherry Mountain (3,554 feet)   *North Country*

This peak appeared on maps as early as 1772 as Pondicherry Mountain, but the origin of that name is obscure. Some people say it is derived from the mountain's proximity to Cherry Pond, but others suggest the name comes from Pondicherry, capitol of French India. The city was a scene of frequent struggles between the French and English, and it has been surmised that the name was given to the mountain by French explorers from Canada. To the north of Cherry Mountain, east of *Whitefield,* is Cherry Pond, with Little Cherry Pond 0.5 mile northwest. See *Pondicherry Notch* and *Pondicherry Wildlife Refuge.*

Chickwolnepy Brook   *Mahoosuc Range Area*

"Frog Pond" is what the name of this brook meant in the Abenaki language. Located northeast of Berlin, it is the only stream in the vicinity to take its rise from a pond. Just to the southeast is 1,945-foot Chickwolnepy Mountain, which until a 1936 USBGN decision had also been called Bickford.

Chocorua, Mount (3,475 feet)   *Chocorua, East Sandwich*

As the *History of Carroll County* says, no other peak has been so celebrated in song, legend, and story. All the legends agree that the peak was named for the Sokosis chief, Chocorua, who lived in the early 1700s. And all agree he met a tragic end on the mountain. The most prosaic of the stories says Chocorua died on the mountain while hunting, apparently by falling from a high rock.

But other tales speak of massacre and vengeance. According to many tales, Chocorua's young son died after eating some poison left out for foxes by white settlers, who had previously enjoyed good neighborly relations with Chocorua. The chief blamed the settlers for his son's death and in revenge slew the wife and children of a settler named Cornelius Campbell. Campbell and others, seeking vengeance in their turn, pursued Chocorua to the mountain's summit, where he was shot. As he lay dying on the rocks, so the story goes, he said to his slayers, "Chocorua goes to the Great Spirit—his curse stays with the white man." Soon after, cattle began dying in the region. This, however, supposedly was traced not to the influence of the chief's malediction but to unusually high concentrations of muriate of lime in the water, and a dose of soapsuds solved the problem.

One variant of the story says Chocorua's son didn't figure in the legend at all. According to this version, Chocorua was pursued up the mountain by white settlers seeking vengeance for an Indian massacre, and Chocorua was not shot but leaped from the peak in defiance of his pursuers.

In 1986 the WMNF designated the Mount Chocorua Scenic Area here.

Chocorua Lake   *Chocorua, East Sandwich*

The same Sokosis chief who gave his name to the mountain (see *Mount Chocorua*) also gave his name to the lake at its base. According to tradition, Indian legend says the lake's stillness was sacred to the Great Spirit, who would sink instantly the canoe of any person daring to shatter the silence by speaking.

Christine Lake   *North Country*

This scenic lake in *Stark* at the base of the *Percy Peaks* in *Stratford* had been called Stratford Pond, Potters Pond, and North Pond. (*South Pond,* now the site of a state park, is across the valley.) But on September 13, 1883, at their first annual meeting, the members of the Percy Summer Club voted to rename the lake in honor of Mrs. Christine Coates of Philadelphia, the first lady visitor to be entertained at the club's camp on the lake.

Church Ponds   *Carrigain, Moat Regions*

Frederick Edwin Church (1826–1900) was an American landscape artist who visited the White Mountains to paint. These ponds on *Pond Brook* southwest of *Bartlett* were named for him. They also have been called Deer Ponds, but the USBGN in 1936 approved the present name. The Church Pond Loop Trail to the ponds starts at the *Passcaconaway* Campground. See *Sabbaday Falls*. The WMNF has created the Church Ponds Research Natural Area here.

Cilley, Mount (2,184 feet)   *Moosilauke Region*

The original settlement of Woodstock (then Peeling) was on this mountain about two miles west of the *Pemigewasset River*. It was named for Gen. Joseph Cilley (1734–99), a native of Nottingham who had a distinguished military career in the Revolutionary War and later was a respected judge and politician. By the Civil War the village named for him was deserted. This mountain still bears his name, however.

Clarksville   *North Country*

The lands comprising this town on the upper Connecticut River originally were part of the Dartmouth College Grants, but in 1792 they were purchased by two Dartmouth graduates for a shilling an acre, or $10,000 for eight square miles, to be paid over a period of time. By 1820 one of the purchasers, Benjamin Clark, had cleared enough of the rich river valley to attract other settlers, who named the town Clarksville in his honor. The name Dartmouth College Grant persisted until 1872, however, when the last of the debt was paid.

Clay, Mount (5,532 feet) *Mount Washington, Southern Ridges*

William Oakes, author of *Scenery of the White Mountains,* published in 1848, named this northern shoulder of *Mount Washington* for the distinguished American statesman, Henry Clay (1777–1852). Though he was not a president, as were the men for whom the surrounding peaks were named, Henry Clay nonetheless was a presidential candidate several times.

Cleveland, Mount (2,397 feet)   *Cannon, Kinsman*

Formerly called Round Mountain, this mountain southeast of the village of Bethlehem was later renamed for President Grover Cleveland, who summered at Tamworth. His two terms, 1885–89 and 1893–97, coincided with a growing awareness of the need for forest preservation, and during his administrations forest reserves were created throughout the nation that later became national forests.

Among President Cleveland's many New Hampshire friends was Col. Henry O. Kent of Lancaster. Colonel Kent was among the commissioners to survey and mark the boundary between New Hampshire and Canada in 1858, and Colonel Kent likely was influential in the naming of Mount Cleveland.

Clinton, Mount (4,310 feet)

Mount Washington, Southern Ridges

See *Mount Pierce.*

Clinton Brook

Mount Washington, Southern Ridges

See *Sebosis Brook.*

Cog Railway

Mount Washington, Southern Ridges

In 1852 Sylvester Marsh, a native of *Campton* and later a resident of *Littleton,* got lost in a storm on *Mount Washington* and concluded there had to be an easier and safer way to reach the summit. An inventor who had made considerable money in the meat-packing industry, Marsh was intrigued by an idea first proposed by Herrick Aiken and his son, Walter, inventors from Franklin, for a cog-driven train. By 1858 Marsh had designed and built a small working model, and not long after he achieved something even more difficult—getting financial backing for an idea many people thought was crazy. In 1865 the Mount Washington Steam Railway Company was formed, with Marsh as president and construction agent. Construction began the next year, and three years later, on July 3, 1869, an engine known as Old Peppersass, for the pepper-shaker shape of its smokestack, made the first trip to the summit. Since then, the Cog Railway has continued to make the 3.25-mile trip from the base station to the summit and has become a popular part of the Mount Washington landscape.

Cold River

Carter, Baldface Ranges

The Cold River heads in *Evans Notch* and flows south. Doubtless descriptive, if hardly inspired, this name is quite old, appearing on the *Chatham* charter map and also in Jeremy Belknap's *Journal* of 1792.

Colebrook North Country

When Gov. Benning Wentworth granted this town on the upper Connecticut River in 1762, he named it Dryden in honor of the English poet and playwright. Gov. John Wentworth regranted the town in 1770, and he changed the name to Colebrook to honor Sir George Colebrook, a relative by marriage and chairman of the board of the British East India Company.

Cole Hill (2,645 feet) *Cannon, Kinsman*

The artist Thomas Cole (1801–48) was a member of the Hudson River School of landscape painters. He came to New Hampshire in the 1830s; his *View in New Hampshire* was exhibited in the Royal Academy in London, and his well-known *The Death of Chocorua* was painted here. This small summit in *Easton,* southwest of *Sugar Hill,* was named for him.

Coleman State Park *North Country*

In 1957, the state purchased 1,573 acres in the town of Stewartstown from the estate of Horace C. Coleman to create this state park; the park was named for him.

Connecticut Lakes *North Country*

These four lakes were named because they are the first major water bodies on the *Connecticut River.* It would seem the actual headwaters of the river should be called First Lake, but it is the other way around; they are *First, Second, Third,* and *Fourth* going north. First Connecticut Lake has been called simply Connecticut Lake, but in 1968 the USBGN recognized the name with the numeral. Third Lake was formerly known as Lake Carmel, for a mountain visible in the northeast, and also Lake Saint Sophia, but again a 1968 USBGN decision established the present name.

Connecticut River *Connecticut Region*

White men's names are on the peaks of the White Mountains, and Indians' names are on the rivers. This is primarily because the Indians were little interested in the mountains, especially as single units, whereas the rivers were vital transportation arteries. The antecedents of the present name Connecticut had varying spellings and pronunciations, mostly because different Indian dialects were spoken along the river, but they all sounded like Connecticut, and they all meant "the long river." A 1713 map published in France spelled the name "counitegou." The present spelling appeared on a map as early as 1760.

Conway   *Carter, Baldface Ranges*

When the first white settlers arrived in this region, they borrowed the name and possibly the site of an already existing Indian village—*Pequawket.* (This name also referred to the subdivision of the Eastern Abenakis who lived along the *Saco River.*) Darby Field called it Pegwagget when he passed through in 1642 on his way to climb *Mount Washington,* and it wasn't long before the name was Anglicized to the unflattering name of Pigwacket.

In 1765 the town was formally named for Henry Seymour Conway (1721–93), a dashing and ambitious younger son of a prominent English family. But hardly had the new name been given when it was mutated to designate different parts of the town; one section was called Conway Street, another Conway Center, and another Conway Corner. Conway Street, an old farming section near Conway Center, was once known as Fag End.

Conway also was called Dolloftown, after an early settler, and an old psalter found in 1774 has the following rhyme in it:

> Thre men went up from dolluf town,
>   And stop ol Nite at Foresters Pockit
> To mak ye Road Bi ingun Hil
>   To git clere up to nort pigogit.
> To Emri's kamp up Kesuk Brok,
>   Wha Chadbun is Beginnen.

Conway Lake   *Carter, Baldface Ranges*

This pond southeast of the village of Conway was originally known as Walkers Pond. As early as 1766 a Capt. Timothy Walker had a grist mill and a sawmill here, and in 1773 he was granted 100 acres of land bordering the pond and its outlet. The county commissioners of Carroll County later changed the name to Conway Lake, but the old name continued to be used for a long time.

Cook Path North Country

Eugene Beauharnais Cook made his first visit to Randolph in 1878 and spent summers for many years at the Ravine House. With other enthusiastic hikers and AMC members of the time, Cook became involved in trail-making—he helped build the Air Line and Valley Way trails—and this path from Randolph Hill Road to Ice Gulch honors his efforts.

Coolidge Mountain, Big (3,294 feet)
Franconia, Twin, Willey Ranges

Coolidge Mountain, Little (2,421 feet)

This ridge northeast of *Lincoln* bears the name of Calvin Cooldige (1872–1933), thirtieth president of the U.S.

Coösauk Fall Mount Washington, Southern Ridges

William H. Peek, early explorer and botanist in the White Mountains, mistakenly thought the Abenaki word "coos" meant "jolt" or "rough," so he joined that with "-auke," the Abenaki suffix meaning "place," to name this rough place on *Bumpus Brook* on *Mount Madison*. See *Coös County*.

Coös County

The largest and northernmost of New Hampshire's ten counties, Coös County takes its name from "coo-ash," an Abenaki word signifying "white pine"; the Western Abenaki Indian group living in the area were known as the "Coo-ash-aukes," or "dwellers in the place of the white pines," the name sometimes also transliterated as Cowasuck. Originally, the "white pine place" was the broad river meadows near Newbury, Vermont, and *Haverhill*; this area was known as "the Cohos." When the meadows near *Lancaster* began to be settled, that area was known as "the Upper Cohoss." And still later, when the area around *Colebrook* was being settled, the famous mapmaker Philip Carrigain bestowed on that region the title of "the Cohoss above the Upper Cohoss." The county was created in 1803, but references to the name appear earlier, and in varied forms. The umlaut over the second "o" signifies it is to be pronounced as a separate syllable, COH-ahs, unlike the name of Coos Bay in Oregon, there spelled without the umlaut and pronounced COOZ.

Coppermine Brook *Cannon, Kinsman*

This brook running northeast from *Kinsman* Ridge received its name from the copper mine on its banks. Copper ore was mined here for many years in the 1800s and smelted in the iron foundry in *Franconia*. See *Ore Hill*.

Crawford (general)

Abel Crawford arrived in the White Mountains in 1791, leaving the flat and fertile farmlands of the *Connecticut River* valley at Guildhall, Vermont, to settle at the site later known as *Fabyan*, at the northern end of what is now *Crawford Notch*, living in a hut built by some settlers whose holdings he had purchased. Abel Crawford soon sold his cabin to his father-in-law, Eleazar Rosebook, and moved twelve miles south, to the site later called *Notchland* in *Harts Location*; he built an inn for travelers that was called the Mount Crawford House. It was here, in the notch in the heart of the White Mountains, that Abel Crawford's son Ethan Allen was born, in 1792, and it was here the boy grew up, helping his father work the land and hunting and fishing in the mountains. As an adult, Ethan Allen stood six foot three inches and was prodigiously strong. In 1811 he left home to enlist in the army and later intended to settle permanently in New York State, but in 1816 he returned at the request of his ailing grandfather, Rosebrook. When the old man died a year later, Ethan Allen inherited the property—and the debts. The same year Ethan Allen and his first cousin, Lucy Howe, were married. The next year, in 1818, the Old Moosehorn Tavern, Ethan Allen and Lucy's home and inn, burned. They rebuilt it. Then the next year Ethan Allen, aided by his father, built the first trail to the summit of Mount Washington; it was named, appropriately, the *Crawford Path*; it began opposite the present Crawford House and is the oldest continually used trail in the White Mountains, still following Ethan Allen's original route most of the way. In 1840 Ethan Allen's brother, Thomas, improved the trail as a bridle path, and Abel, then seventy-five, was the first to ride a horse to the summit.

As a guide in the White Mountains, Ethan Allen had no equals. He introduced many of the early botanical explorers to the mountains, and in 1820 he accompanied Philip Carrigain and the other members of the Weeks-Brackett party when they named most of the *Presidential* peaks. In 1821 he guided the first women up Mount Washington. The same year he built the first structure on Mount

Washington's summit, a place to shelter the guests he guided there; in 1823 he constructed three stone huts.

But, despite his labors and his fame, Ethan Allen and Lucy always were in financial difficulty; once creditors had him jailed in *Lancaster.* Finally, in 1837, tired and broke, he left the White Mountains for Guildhall, from whence his father had come. He sold his inn to Horace Fabyan (see *Fabyan*). Yet, as when he left the White Mountains earlier, his absence was temporary. In 1843 Ethan Allen and Lucy returned; he rented the White Mountain House, a mile from his former home. Here he died three years later, aged fifty-four. He was known as the Giant of the Hills. Five years later Abel Crawford, called the Patriarch of the Mountains, died, aged eighty-five. Lucy Crawford survived her husband for twenty-three years, dying in 1869. In 1846 she published *The History of the White Mountains from the First Settlement of Upper Coos and Pequaket,* based on her diary. The passing of the Crawfords marked the end of an era in the White Mountains, but the mark they made on White Mountains history is as permanent as are the many features bearing their name.

Crawford, Mount (3,129 feet)
Mount Washington, Southern Ridges

Dr. Samuel Bemis, who lived in *Crawford Notch* and was intimately connected with the Crawford family, suggested that this peak be named for Abel Crawford and his son Ethan Allen, early settlers, explorers, and guides.

Crawford Notch
Franconia, Twin, Willey Ranges

Before Abel Crawford came to the huge defile later to bear his name, Crawford Notch was known as The White Mountain Notch or simply The Notch. The notch is said to have been discovered by Europeans in April 1771 when, according to tradition, thirty-year-old Capt. Timothy Nash became lost while following a moose through dense forest on a mountain. Climbing a tree to get his bearings, he saw to the south the huge cleft in the mountains later to be called Crawford Notch. (Nash lost a mitten during this incident, resulting in the mountain being called Mount *Mitten* .) For years the settlers of *Lancaster* and nearby towns had yearned to take their trade goods to Portsmouth or Portland via *Conway,* but the White Mountains barred their way; instead they had to travel fifty miles down the *Connecticut River* to *Haverhill,* an easy journey down but a difficult one back, and farther from the desired markets. In 1767 the possibility of a route through the White Mountains was discussed at a meeting of Lancaster's proprietors; Nash was at that meeting. So when Nash spied Crawford Notch on that April day more than two hundred years ago, he had reason to forget about his mitten. Nash and Benjamin Sawyer the next year undertook to prove that a horse could be taken through the notch, but when they had to lower the horse over a cliff with a rope, they also demonstrated how difficult transportation through the notch was (see *Nash and Sawyers Location*). Abel Crawford built a path that made the notch accessible to the many explorers who were to follow, and he provided them with accommodations when they came. Abel Crawford lived most of his life in the White Mountains; he explored them, he built roads and trails through them, and he guided and assisted travelers in them. Few persons have had so beautiful and awesome a place named for them, and few have deserved it more than Abel Crawford.

Crawford Path   *Mount Washington, Southern Ridges*

After several parties had visited *Mount Washington*, Abel Crawford and his son Ethan Allen saw clearly that a path was needed, so they built one. It was said to be the first path up Mount Washington, and today it still follows very closely the original route. Begun in 1819, it was first called the Mount Washington Path, but as other paths to the summit appeared this path came to be known instead for its builders.

Crawfords Purchase   *Mount Washington, Southern Ridges*

In 1834 this unincorporated tract of land east of *Fabyan* and *Bretton Woods* was granted to Ethan Allen Crawford and Thomas and Nathaniel Abbott for $8,000, or less than sixty cents an acre. The land now includes many of the approaches to the Mount Washington *Cog Railway*.

Crescent, Mount (3,230 feet)   *North Country*

The shape of its summit is responsible for the name of this mountain in the *Crescent Range* in the town of *Randolph*. It is referred to on an old USGS map as Randolph Mountain, but that name more accurately now appears on a summit to the southwest. A 3,265-foot mountain in the range 2.75 miles northeast of this peak also had been called Mount Crescent, but in 1936 the USBGN approved the name

Black Crescent Mountain for that summit and Mount Crescent for this.

Crescent Range *North Country*

This small group mostly in the town of *Randolph* takes its name from one of its two principal summits, but it is not certain which. Most likely is *Mount Crescent,* 3,230 feet, at the south end of the range, just northeast of the community of Randolph Hill and linked by trail with nearby *Mount Randolph. Black Crescent Mountain,* formerly also called Crescent Mountain, at 3,265 feet is slightly higher, but it is more inconspicuous and less easily accessible. The mountains have also been known as the Randolph Range, but a 1936 USBGN decision established Crescent Range as the accepted form.

The Crippies *Mount Washington, Southern Ridges*

These are four small humps north of *Mount Pickering.* Why they have this unusual name is unknown.

Crystal *North Country*

Proximity to Crystal Fall is the most likely reason for the name of this village in the town of *Stark.*

Crystal Cascade *Mount Washington, Southern Ridges*

The *Ellis River* once was known as the Crystal River, and this fall near the outlet of *Tuckerman Ravine* once shared that name. It appeared as Crystal Falls on Bond's map of 1853 and as Crystal Cascade in Rev. Thomas Starr King's book of 1859, where he wrote that the waterfall's descent reminded him of "graceful and perpetual youth."

Culhane Brook *Northern Peaks, Great Gulf*

The Culhanes, the Barnes, and the Copps were three early families in this area, and their names are preserved on the *Dolly Copp Campground,* the *Barnes Field Campground,* and this brook heading on *Mount Madison* and flowing easterly to the *Peabody River.*

Currier Mountain (2,790 feet) *North Country*

Horace C. Currier (1879–1943) was a USFS employee who began work in the WMNF in 1912 and was noted for his sound forestry practices. The mountain in the *Dartmouth Range* west and slightly north of *Mount Mitten* was named for him; it previously had been called Pine Peak.

Cushman, Mount (3,105 feet) *Moosilauke Region*

Nathaniel Cushman was an early settler in the town of *Woodstock,* and he gave his name to this mountain. The name first appeared on Philip Carrigain's map of 1816.

Cutler River *Mount Washington, Southern Ridges*

Manasseh Cutler, born in Connecticut in 1742, was a Yale graduate, engaged in whaling, became a lawyer, studied theology, and eventually was minister at Hamilton, Massachusetts, near Ipswich, until his death in 1823. He also studied and practiced medicine and was an enthusiastic meteorologist and botanist, and it was as a botanist that he became a member of Dr. Jeremy Belknap's 1784 expedition to the White Mountains. Belknap's party followed this stream draining *Tuckerman Ravine* in their ascent of *Mount Washington,* and it was named for Cutler. Cutler was among numerous botanists who explored the White Mountains—he was the first to describe Mount Washington's alpine vegetation—and whose names appear on natural features. Cutler climbed Mount Washington again in 1804 and at that time estimated the mountain's elevation at 7,055 feet—certainly more accurate that the 10,000-foot estimate of the earlier expedition!

Cutts Grant *Mount Washington, Southern Ridges*

Thomas Cutts of Maine was granted these lands above *Crawford Notch* and adjacent to *Mount Washington* in 1818. Like similar early grants, it is now part of the WMNF.

D

Dalton (town), Mountain (2,142 feet) *Connecticut Region*

This town on the *Connecticut River* once was part of what is now *Littleton*. By 1764 the entire area was known as Chiswick, then in 1770 as Apthorp, and in 1784 as Dalton, in honor of Tristram Dalton, one of New England's foremost colonial merchants. Dalton Mountain, a ridge running east and west the length of the town, is named for the town.

Daniel Webster—Scout Trail *Northern Peaks, Great Gulf*

This trail leading from the *Dolly Copp Campground* to connect with the *Osgood Trail* at Osgood Junction below the *Mount Madison* summit was cut in 1933 by members of the Daniel Webster Boy Scout Council. See also *Mount Webster.*

Dartmouth, Mount (3,721 feet) *North Country*
Dartmouth Range

In 1876, New Hampshire state geologist Charles H. Hitchcock proposed naming this peak near *Cherry Mountain* for Dartmouth College, where Hitchcock also was professor of geology and mineralogy, a position he held for forty years. Ironically, Dartmouth also was the original name of the town of *Jefferson,* where the mountain is located. Mount Dartmouth is the highest summit of the Dartmouth Range, whose other main summit is *Mount Deception.*

Davis Brook, Path; Mount (3,800 feet)

Mount Washington, Southern Ridges

The history of *Crawford Notch* is largely a family affair. Nathaniel T. P. Davis, manager of the Mount Crawford House, married Hannah Crawford and thus became son-in-law of Abel Crawford, patriarch of the region and pioneer trailbuilder. Davis wanted to build his own bridle path up *Mount Washington,* so he started at Bemis, near the hotel he managed. The path wound up *Bemis Ridge,* to *Montalban Ridge,* and on to Mount Washington. It opened in 1845 and was the third bridle path built to the summit.

The path lost popularity over the years with the arrival of the carriage road and the *Cog Railway.* In 1910, however, it was reopened as a footpath, and today it follows closely Davis's original route. See *Mount Resolution.*

Dead Diamond River

North Country

See *Diamond.*

Deception Brook; Mount (3,700 feet)   *North Country*
Deception, Little Mount (2,435 feet)

In August 1823, three men from a party staying at the Mount Crawford House set out to climb *Mount Washington,* leaving the women in their group behind. The women, to amuse themselves, set out to climb what appeared to be an easy and scenic hill to the north. The climb turned out to be much longer and more difficult than they had anticipated, and one of them suggested the name Mount Deception for the mountain. Little Mount Deception is just south of Mount Deception, while Deception Brook heads on Mount Deception's west slopes and flows west and then south into the *Ammonoosuc River;* until a 1936 USBGN decision, this brook also had been known as Cherry Mountain Brook and White House Brook.

Deer Hill (1,367 feet)   *Speckled Mountain Region*
Deer Hill, Little (1,090 feet)

One of literally hundreds of similarly named features throughout the U.S., this summit south of *Speckled Mountain,* east of *Cold River,* sometimes is called Big Deer; Little Deer Hill is to the west.

Desolation Pond · *Mount Washington, Southern Ridges*

No connection exists between this tiny pond nestled beneath the ridge separating *Mounts Eisenhower* and *Franklin* and the Desolation Trail in the *Pemigewasset Wilderness*—except their bleak names. The specific origin of this name is unknown.

Devils Den · *Franconia, Twin, Willey Ranges*

Among early White Mountains settlers and explorers, the talk was that a cave on the sheer cliffs of *Mount Willard* was littered with bones. The cave was called Devils Den. Franklin Leavitt, the folk mapmaker and versifier from *Lancaster,* was said to have been lowered into the cave from above on a rope; he saw bones in the cave and refused to enter. In 1870, a USGS party mustered the courage to enter the dreaded cave—and found nothing.

Devils Hopyard · *North Country*

Some early visitors to this rugged natural ravine near *South Pond* State Park in *Stark* were reminded of a hopyard by the vines hanging from trees on the ledges. It is a wild and sunless place; thus the name Devils Hopyard evolved.

Devils Kitchen · *Northern Peaks, Great Gulf*

Bumpus Brook here passes through a narrow and fascinating gorge, where the tumult when the stream is in spate likely inspired the name.

Devils Slide · *North Country*

This conspicuous cliff, hanging like a stage backdrop behind the village of *Stark,* received its name from an Indian legend. The Indians peopled the mountains with invisible spirits, who warred frequently. During one particularly tumultuous battle, one half of a mountain blocking the valley of the Upper *Ammonoosuc River* subsided into the earth, leaving the valley as it appears today.

Diamond Ponds, River, Ridge (approx. 2,800 feet) · *North Country*

A moose, not a mineral, gave these North Country features their names. A man named Isaac Diamond, while hunting between the ponds in 1778, shot and wounded a large bull moose. The moose charged him, nearly tearing off his clothes. Diamond dodged behind a tree; the moose kept coming; Diamond fled to another tree; and finally, after reloading his rifle, he shot and killed the moose. From this incident a river, a ridge, and two ponds received their names. The Swift Diamond River and the Dead Diamond River were named for their currents.

Dianas Baths   *Carrigain, Moat Regions*

These curious circular stone cavities on Lucy Brook originally were known as the Home of the Water Fairies; tradition says evil water sprites inhabited the ledges, tormenting the Sokosis Indians until a mountain god answered the Indians' prayers and swept the sprites away in a flood. But sometime before 1859 a Miss Hubbard of Boston, a guest at the old Mount Washington House in North Conway, rechristened them Dianas Baths, presumably to evoke images of the Roman nature goddess. The pools are also called *Lucys Baths.*

Dixville (town), Notch, Peak (3,482 feet)   *North Country*

Col. Timothy Dix and his son, Col. Timothy Dix, Jr., in 1805 purchased nearly 30,000 acres in the area of this rugged notch, and in 1811 they were authorized by legislation to construct a roadway through the notch to the Maine border. The project was completed under the supervision of Daniel Webster and his brother Ezekiel, who were then lawyers for Colonel Dix in Boscawen. Dixville Notch— with its jagged cliffs, near-alpine lake, ski area, and stately hotel— today calls itself Little Switzerland, but to the early settlers it must have seemed like "Little Perdition." Until 1815, John and Betsy Whittemore were the first and only settlers of the region. They stuck it out three years, until Betsy died and John decided to move to *Colebrook.* The road was not kept open in the winter, and John had to keep his wife's body frozen all winter before he could bury her in the spring. Living conditions in the notch have improved considerably since then.

Dodge Cutoff   *Cannon, Kinsman*

This short trail connecting the Hi-Cannon Trail with the *Lonesome Lake* Trail honors Joe Dodge, former manager of the AMC hut system.

Dodge Pond   *Connecticut Region*

David Dodge, born in 1760 in New Boston, married Letty Tallent
and moved to Dodges Falls while still a young man. He became a
citizen of *Lyman* before 1800, locating on Moulton Hill, but he later
moved to the pond bearing his name, where he died in 1848.

Dollof Pond   *Carter, Baldface Ranges*

Dollof Pond, like Dolloftown, an early name for *Conway*, took its
name from an early settler named Dollof.

Dolly Copp Campground   *Northern Peaks, Great Gulf*

Dolly Copp began life as Dolly Emery, from Bartlett, Maine, but
in 1831, while still in her teens, she married Hayes D. Copp, of Stowe,
Maine, and together they built a farm in the wilderness, the site of
which is now this campground in the WMNF. They lived here for
nineteen years and raised four children before they had any close
neighbors.

Dolly of necessity was self-reliant, and throughout her married life
she made all her own apparel—except shoes. She had tiny feet, and
she imported shoes from Portland, Maine. She was famous for her
handcrafted linen and woolen articles, and when the *Glen House*
opened in 1852 many visitors came to her farmstead. She smoked a
short clay pipe.

It is said that soon after her fiftieth wedding anniversary she an-
nounced, "Hayes is well enough, and fifty years is long enough to live
with any man." Whereupon the aged couple peacefully divided their
possessions, and she departed to live in Auburn, Maine, with a
daughter. Hayes returned to his native Stowe, Maine.

Doublehead, Mount (3,050 and 2,938 feet)
Carter, Baldface Ranges

The name of this mountain northeast of *Jackson* comes from the
peak having two summits: North Doublehead, 3,050 feet, and South
Doublehead, 2,938 feet. The mountain was called by this name on
Belknap's map of 1791. There is another Mount Doublehead in the
Squam Range.

Double Top Mountain (1,900 feet)   *North Country*

Descriptively named summit south of *Lake Umbagog*.

Drake Brook, Ravine, Trail *Waterville Valley Region*

Arnold Drake settled in *Waterville Valley* about 1840; these features were named for him.

Dry River *Mount Washington, Southern Ridges*

This watercourse, heading in *Oakes Gulf* on the south side of *Mount Washington* and running south-southeast to join the *Saco River* at the Dry River Campground, also has been called the Mount Washington River, but, as the AMC guide puts it, "Dry River has won the battle, possibly because of the irony of the name. . . . Though in a dry season the flow is meager, with lots of rocks lying uncovered, its watershed has extremely rapid runoff, and its sudden floods are legendary."

Dryad Brook, Fall *Mahoosuc Range Area*

Like many features in the White Mountains, this short brook takes its name from classical mythology, wherein a dryad was a tree nymph who lived in the trees and died when the trees died. The brook heads north of *Bald Cap Peak* and runs into *Austin Mill Brook*. Dryad Fall is on this brook.

Ducks Head *Mount Washington, Southern Ridges*

See *Iron Mountain*.

Dugway Campground *Carrigain, Moat Regions*

This recreation site on the *Swift River* west of *Conway* village was named because it is near the "dugway" portion of the old Swift River Road, located on the north side of the river. "Dugway" simply means "dug into the bank."

Dummer *North Country*

A famous fort, a famous academy, and a sparsely populated northern New Hampshire town all were named for the same person—William Dummer, governor of Massachusetts. Fort Dummer on the *Connecticut River* in Massachusetts is said to have been the earliest and most famous of New England "Indian Forts." And Governor Dummer Academy in Massachusetts was a famous colonial private academy. The town of Dummer in the North Country was granted in 1773 and incorporated in 1848.

Durand Ridge

Northern Peaks, Great Gulf

John Durand was a member of the London Board of Trade and as such had association with the shipping interests of the colonial governor, John Wentworth. Governor Wentworth was fond of naming towns for political and business associates, and in 1772 he gave to what is now the town of *Randolph* the name of Durand. The town bore that name until 1824, when it received its present name. The White Mountains enthusiast William H. Peek knew the history of Randolph and named this prominent ridge of *Mount Adams* for the early name of the town.

Durgin Mountain (2,404 feet)

Speckled Mountain Region

Levi Durgin was one of six very early settlers near this mountain immediately northeast of *Speckled Mountain*.

Durgin Pond

Chocorua, East Sandwich

James Holmes Durgin and his wife, Jane Varney Durgin, were Quakers whose home was a stopping point on the Underground Railroad for escaped slaves. James had a gristmill beside the Durgin covered bridge, and Jane taught in the schoolhouse opposite the bridge. The Durgins eventually moved away, but not before they gave their name to this pond south of the village of Madison and a clock to the church in Madison. Jane is buried in a nearby cemetery.

Eagle Cliff *Franconia, Twin, Willey Ranges*

This spur of *Mount Lafayette* received its name in 1858 when Rev. Thomas Hill discovered an eagles' nest here.

Eagle Mountain (1,615 feet) *Carter, Baldface Regions*

This low peak forming the south end of the ridge running from *Wildcat Mountain* derived its name from its upper crags, once the abode of eagles described by Moses F. Sweetser as "bold and rapacious."

Eastman Brook *Waterville Valley Region*

Amos Eastman was a hunter killed by Indians near *Baker River*; this brook west of *Mounts Osceola* and *Tecumseh* possibly was named for him.

Eastman Mountain (2,936 feet) *Carter, Baldface Regions*

This peak south of *South Baldface* most likely received its name because the Eastman family homestead was nearby.

Easton *Cannon, Kinsman*

The name of this sparsely settled town near Franconia appears to be a corruption of "eastern." Until 1867 the town was known as Eastern Landaff, but in that year it was incorporated as Easton.

Echo Lake   *Carrigain, Moat Regions*

Having the cliffs of White Horse Ledge as a backdrop doubtless facilitates sounds echoing across this lake west of North Conway.

Echo Lake   *Franconia, Twin, Willey Ranges*

Hundreds of Echo Lakes exist throughout the nation, and they all have the same origin for their names: sounds echo freely across them. From the center of this Echo Lake in *Franconia Notch* at the base of *Eagle Cliff,* conversations are said to echo two or three times, and, according to tradition, Indians regarded these reverberating sounds as the war whoops of the gods.

Edmands Col, Path   *Northern Peaks, Great Gulf*
Edmands Path   *Mount Washington, Southern Ridges*

Although dozens of men and organizations have cut trails in the White Mountains, no man is more responsible for the present system of hiking paths than Prof. J. Rayner Edmands. Throughout his long life, he labored tirelessly to make the beauty and grandeur of the White Mountains accessible to his fellow hikers.

Born in 1850, Edmands first visited the White Mountains in 1868 while still a student at the Massachusetts Institute of Technology. He stayed at Jefferson Highlands, and with several other youths he ascended *Cascade Ravine,* naming several of the waterfalls en route. He joined the AMC when it was founded in 1876, immediately assuming positions of responsibility within the club; he became the AMC's president in 1886, and from 1894 to his death in 1910 he was one of the AMC's trustees of real estate. He was a professor at Harvard Observatory, and with Prof. E. T. Quimby he triangulated *Mount Washington* for the U.S. Coast and Geodetic Survey; during the summers of 1880 and 1881 they worked out of a tower specially constructed on top of Mount Washington.

But it is for his tireless trailbuilding in the White Mountains that Edmands is most often remembered. Edmands mountaineered in the Rockies in 1888 and 1890, and he was impressed by the system of well-graded trails the miners had created there. He returned to the White Mountains determined to create a similar system of trails. He began working in the summer of 1891, going into Cascade Ravine, where he built a shelter, and blazing a trail up Emerald Tongue, the ridge he renamed *Israel Ridge.* By the next year he had created a system of cairns above timberline whereby hikers could find their way even during heavy fog. The next few years were occupied with constructing trails in the northern peaks, as well as numerous pleasure paths around *Randolph* and *Jefferson*. When logging operations threatened to destroy much of his work on the northern peaks, he shifted his base of operations to the southern peaks, but he did not forsake Jefferson and Randolph, for he negotiated with the lumber barons to have their loggers preserve the trails he had created. Even when he was an old man, his trailmaking continued unabated, and in some years he spent on trailmaking more money from his personal account than was contributed from the AMC treasury.

Edmands died in 1910, just a year after constructing the Edmands Path. His goal throughout his long years in the White Mountains was to create trails and facilities that would make hiking possible for persons of all abilities. His trails survive today, and the use they receive is proof of his success. A bronze tablet commemorating Edmands is at the col named for him.

Eisenhower, Mount (4,761 feet)
Mount Washington, Southern Ridges

When the Weeks-Brackett party ascended *Mount Washington* in 1820 to name the high peaks for the nation's presidents, they encountered a problem—not enough presidents. They stepped out of the presidential league to give *Mount Franklin* its name, but when they came to the next peak they were stumped. Finally, and perhaps under the influence of the "O-be-joyful" they had imbibed, they gave this mountain southwest of Mount Franklin the name Mount Pleasant. According to the White Mountains explorer Prof. Edward Tuckerman, this peak in the southern *Presidential Range* was called Dome Mountain before being christened Mount Pleasant; the USGS later called it Pleasant Dome. In 1824, in the *American Journal of Science,* James Pierce called it Mount Prospect. By 1969, the nation had had presidents in abundance, and in the year that he died, Dwight David Eisenhower's name was added to the pantheon of presidents honored in the White Mountains; Sherman Adams, former New Hampshire governor and assistant to President Eisenhower, assisted greatly in this effort. After waiting the required one year following a person's death before approving an honorific name, the USBGN approved the name Mount Eisenhower in 1970. The formal dedication ceremony was held in 1972 at Eisenhower Wayside Park on U.S. Route 302. Ironically, the earlier name survives on Mount Pleasant Brook.

Elbow Pond   *Moosilauke Region*

Tradition says that one Thomas Vincent, a former Revolutionary War soldier who in 1875 settled south of *Woodstock* Center, was hunting one fall on *Mount Cushman* when he spied a pond below. Returning home, he said the pond had been shaped like an elbow, hence the name.

Elephant Head   *Mount Washington, Southern Ridges*

This ledge outside the north "gateway" to *Crawford Notch* was named because white quartz veins in gray rock resemble an elephant's head. Lucy Crawford referred to the ledge by this name in her diary.

Elizabeth Mountain (approx. 2,050 feet)
Speckled Mountain Region

Forming the west flank of *Miles Notch,* this mountain was named for Elizabeth, daughter of E. Lester Jones, director of the U.S. Coast and Geodetic Survey, who owned land in the area.

Ellis River   *Mount Washington, Southern Ridges*

The origin of this name is unknown, but it has associated with it a charming legend. An Indian family living near the river's headwaters had a daughter possessed of such beauty and virtue that no brave in the area could pass as an acceptable mate for her. One day she suddenly disappeared, and, when she was not found, the whole tribe mourned. Later some hunters searching the mountains for game discovered the lost maiden. She was sitting on the shore of the clear mountain stream with a youth whose hair, like hers, floated below his waist. The couple vanished as soon as they became aware of the hunters. But the girl's parents, hearing the tale, knew their daughter's companion to be one of the kindly spirits of the mountain, and they began considering him their son. And he acknowledged the kinship, for they had only to call upon him and he would provide them with game.

The river, formed by the confluence of the *Cutler River* and the *New River,* seems to have been named Ellis River, or Ellis's River for as long as maps have given a name to the river. The earliest mention of the name found thus far is in the grant of land to Philip Bailey, written in 1770. Moses F. Sweetser speculated the original spelling may have been Elise or Elis.

Ellsworth (village), Pond *Moosilauke Region*

This village west of Campton has had two names in its history, and both honored men who played important roles in the geographical development of early America. The first name was Trecothick—the only Trecothick anywhere in the U.S.—and it came from Barlow Trecothick, Lord Mayor of London and head of the British East India Company. He and others induced the crown authorities to establish New Hampshire as a separate province with its own governors, free from Massachusetts, under whose jurisdiction it had been for years. In 1802 the town was incorporated under the name of Ellsworth, for Chief Justice Oliver Ellsworth of Connecticut. That year Justice Ellsworth had negotiated the peace treaty with France that resulted in the Louisiana Purchase.

Errol *North Country*

This town and its name are an odd match. Most of the town is forested wilderness, including within its boundaries the *Androscoggin* and *Diamond Rivers* and several large North Country lakes. From these—through logging and outdoor recreation—the village derives its subsistence. It always has been a rugged, frontier sort of place.

Yet its name comes from a refined aristocratic figure in British history. In 1774 Gov. John Wentworth chartered the town as Errol after James Hay of Scotland, Fifteenth Earl of Errol, owner of Linlithgow Castle, birthplace of Mary Queen of Scots and King James V. The town was incorporated in 1836.

Ervings Location *North Country*

This tract of wilderness southwest of *Dixville Notch* was granted in 1775 to Capt. William Erving of Boston, a soldier in the French and Indian Wars.

Ethan Pond *Franconia, Twin, Willey Ranges*

Around 1830 Ethan Allen Crawford discovered this pond southwest of *Mount Willey* while he was on one of his many trapping trips, and it was named for him. It sometimes is called Ethans Pond, and it has been called Willey Pond, because of its proximity to Mount Willey, but the name approved by the USBGN in 1949 is Ethan Pond.

Evans Brook, Notch   *Carter, Baldface Ranges*

Capt. John Evans was one of the original grantees of Fryeburg,
Maine, and an experienced Indian fighter. He had been one of Roger's
Rangers, and in August 1781, following an Indian raid on Bethel,
Maine, he was placed in command of an armed guard on the *An-
droscoggin River* until winter removed the danger of attack. Earlier,
in 1774, he had worked on the first road through *Pinkham Notch*.
Later, in 1784, he guided Dr. Jeremy Belknap on his White Moun-
tains expedition.

It also is possible, however, that the brook and the notch were
named for the Amos Evans family, who were settlers here as early as
1832.

The first road through Evans Notch was attempted in 1861, when
a narrow road for horse-drawn vehicles was constructed between
North Chatham and Gilead, Maine, following what was probably an
Indian trail. In hardly a year it had washed out, and the route was
only a hiking trail until 1914, when the USFS began upgrading it, a
task they completed in 1936 with help from the Civilian Conservation Corps.

Fabyan

Franconia, Twin, Willey Ranges

Fabyans Path

Mount Washington, Southern Ridges

Horace Fabyan's inn was among the most famous in the White Mountains, and from it comes the name of this historic site on U.S. Route 302. Fabyan was a provisions dealer from Maine, and in 1837 he bought from Ethan Allen Crawford the inn at the northern approach to *Crawford Notch*. He called it the Mount Washington House, and he listed among its features his famous six-foot tin horn that he blew each day at sundown. (Just down the road Tom Crawford set off a cannon daily.)

But the site of Fabyan's inn was well known long before Fabyan arrived here. It was known as Giants Grave because of a large earth formation resembling a giant burial mound. In 1791 Abel Crawford bought out the holdings of some settlers and set up bachelor quarters in one of their huts. This was occupied the next year by Eleazer Rosebrook, father-in-law of Abel Crawford and grandfather of both Ethan Allen and Lucy Crawford. Rosebrook built a rude teamsters' tavern here in 1803, but it burned. Local legend had it that the site was haunted by an Indian who had declared, "No paleface shall take root here; the Great Spirit whispered in my ear."

It apparently was a potent curse, because when Ethan Allen Crawford put up an inn here in 1817 it burned the next year. In 1819 Ethan Allen Crawford built a two-story tavern on the site, but it too burned. Fabyan's Mount Washington House lasted thirty years, until 1869, before the curse seemingly claimed it too. In 1872–73 the Giants Grave was leveled and a large hotel built to accommodate four hundred guests was constructed. Eventually fire claimed it also, in 1951.

The site known as Fabyan was never incorporated, though it has appeared repeatedly on maps since 1879. Fabyan improved a seven-mile bridle path along the *Ammonoosuc River* to the foot of *Mount Washington,* which became known as the Fabyan Turnpike, then later as Fabyans Path. Traces of the path can still be seen from points along the Mount Washington *Cog Railway.* The area separating the southern peaks of the White Mountains from the much lower Cherry-Dartmouth Range is called the Fabyan Plain.

Farlow Ridge   *Chocorua, East Sandwich*

Numerous geological features in the White Mountains were named for botanists. William G. Farlow (1884–1919) was a professor of botany at Harvard University, serving as assistant to the famous Asa Gray. Professor Farlow specialized in mycology, the study of mushrooms and other fungi, and this ridge southwest of *Mount Chocorua* was one of his favorite collecting areas. He had a summer home in Chocorua. The USBGN approved the name in 1924.

Field, Mount (4,326 feet)   *Franconia, Twin, Willey Ranges*

This peak west of *Crawford Notch,* northwest of *Mount Willey,* was at one time known as Mount Lincoln, but later, to avoid confusion with the peak in the *Franconia Range,* it was renamed to honor Darby Field, who in 1642 became the first white man to climb *Mount Washington.*

First Connecticut Lake   *North Country*

See *Connecticut Lakes.*

Fisher Mountain (2,609 feet)   *Waterville Valley*

This summit west of *Waterville Valley* is said to recall Dr. Joshua Fisher (1748–1823), a Massachusetts physician who was a member of Dr. Jeremy Belknap's 1784 expedition to the White Mountains that climbed *Mount Washington.*

Fishin' Jimmy Trail   *Cannon, Kinsman*

The real name of Fishin' Jimmy, for whom this trail to *Lonesome Lake* was named, was James Whitcher, and he was born in *Franconia.* But from personal recollections of him by Annie Trumbull Slosson, who wrote a book about him, Fishin' Jimmy is the name he would have preferred. He was a kindly soul, who found both serenity and wisdom fishing in the brooks of the White Mountains. Once when Mrs. Slosson asked him if he liked fishing, he replied, "You wouldn't ask me if I liked my mother—or my wife."

Fishin' Jimmy died, an old man, after he had fallen while hiking to help rescue two boys who had gotten into trouble on *Mount Lafayette*. The fall occurred as Jimmy stopped to assist his faithful dog, Dash. His death was widely mourned in the area.

Fletcher Fall   *North Country*

Ebenezer Fletcher, recognizing this waterfall on the upper Connecticut River in Pittsburg to be a natural site for a mill, built one here in 1811. The Fletcher operations prospered, and the fall was named for him.

Fletchers Cascade   *Waterville Valley Region*

On Flat Mountain is a fall named, most likely, for Arthur Fletcher of Concord who came to Waterville Valley in the 1870s. The trail to the cascade, probably opened about this time, was destroyed by logging before 1900. It was reopened in 1951.

The Flume   *Franconia, Twin, Willey Ranges*

It has been called perhaps the most beautiful cascade in the world, and Lucy Crawford in her *History of the White Mountains* wrote, "This natural curiosity fills the beholder with amazement and admiration." But its name simply states what it is—a rock flume, awesome and huge. According to tradition, it was discovered in 1808 by ninety-three-year-old Aunt Jessie Guernsey; an inveterate fisherwoman, she came across it in her wanderings. (Another version says she discovered the Flume one night while looking with a tin lantern for a lost cow.)

In 1883, an avalanche dislodged a huge boulder that had been blocking a constriction in the Flume; the boulder's path deepened the watercourse and created two new waterfalls. The stream flowing through The Flume is called Flume Brook.

Flume Mountain (4,327 feet)

Franconia, Twin, Willey Ranges

Flume Mountain, named because Flume Brook flows from it, was originally referred to as one of the *Haystacks,* as was nearby Mount Liberty. Early settlers called them this, doubtless because of their resemblance to haystacks.

The Fool Killer

Chocorua, East Sandwich

Only by looking very carefully on a clear day can a hiker at *Passaconaway* Campground on the *Kancamagus Highway* distinguish a ridge whose north slope visually blends closely with that of North *Tripyramid.* Parties have ascended this ridge, thinking they were ascending Tripyramid, only to discover at the top that a long, deep valley and another ridge lay between them and their goal. The Fool Killer, thus, is an appropriate name for the deceptive ridge.

Forist, Mount (2,046 feet)

North Country

The cliffs of this mountain form a dramatic backdrop on the west for the city of *Berlin,* and the mountain was named for a man prominent in Berlin, Merrill C. Forist. In addition to holding numerous town and state offices, he also ran the Mount Forist Hotel, built around 1866. Locally the mountain sometimes is called Elephant Mountain, because of its shape as seen from Berlin; the summit is at the head.

Francis, Lake

North Country

The largest water body in northern New Hampshire, Lake Francis was named for Francis P. Murphy, who was elected governor in 1937 and was in office while the dam creating the lake was built.

Franconia Brook, Falls

Franconia, Twin, Willey Ranges

Franconia Brook heads east of Franconia Notch, in Franconia, on the southeast slopes of *Mount Garfield* and flows south to join the East Branch of the *Pemigewasset River.* The falls take their name from the brook.

Franconia (town), Notch, Range

Franconia, Twin, Willey Ranges

This region was known as Franconia very early, supposedly for its resemblance to the Franconian Alps in Germany. When Jesse Searle and others were granted lands here in 1764, they called their hopeful settlement Franconia, but the grantees failed to attract enough settlers to build the required thirty houses, so the grant was revoked. The town was regranted in 1772—with allowances for "unimprovable lands, mountains, and waters"—and it was renamed Morristown, after Corbyn Morris of Boston, one of the original grantees, but the name reverted to Franconia in 1782 after much litigation.

Frankenstein Cliff

Franconia, Twin, Willey Ranges

People often assume these cliffs on the west side of *Crawford Notch* were named either for their towering size or their malice toward climbers and hikers, but the name actually has nothing at all to do with the famous monster created in fiction by Mary Shelley. The cliff was named by Dr. Samuel Bemis for Godfrey Nicholas Frankenstein, a young artist who spent much time in the White Mountains and was fascinated by their rugged beauty. Born in Germany in 1820, Frankenstein immigrated to the U.S. in 1831; he began his career as a sign painter in Ohio. He first visited the White Mountains in 1847, camping in Crawford Notch, but later he returned often to paint and to visit Dr. Bemis.

Franklin, Mount (5,004 feet)

Mount Washington, Southern Ridges

When the Weeks-Brackett party from *Lancaster* in 1820 named the high peaks of the White Mountains for U.S. presidents (see *Presidential Range*), they soon faced the problem of having more peaks than presidents, so they named this summit southwest of *Mount Monroe* for an American leader of comparable prestige—Benjamin Franklin.

French Brook

Mahoosuc Range Area

This short south-flowing brook, joining the *Androscoggin* west of *Gilead*, was named for the early French family here.

Fulling Mill Mountain (3,450 feet)   *Mahoosuc Range Area*

A fulling mill was a machine for compacting and shrinking woolen cloth, using heat and moisture. Why this wilderness peak east of *Mahoosuc Notch* bears this name is unknown.

F

Gale River
Franconia, Twin, Willey Ranges

The origins of this name are obscure. A Mr. Gale once sent a gun
to Ethan Allen Crawford from Boston, but no suggestion has been
made that the river flowing northwest from *South Twin Mountain*
was named for him. The name appears on Bond's 1853 map of the
White Mountains. The river's upper reaches are divided into the
South Branch Gale River, which heads on the north slope of Garfield
Ridge and flows north, and the North Branch Gale River, which heads
on the west slopes of the Twin Mountains and also flows north. The
main Gale River joins the *Ammonoosuc River* south of *Littleton*.
Galehead Hut, on a little hump on *Garfield* Ridge, was built by the
AMC in 1932.

Gardner Mountain (2,330 feet)
Connecticut Region

Rev. Andrew Gardner was an early grantee and settler of the town
of *Bath*. He moderated the first town meeting and came to be known
as the town's "patron saint." This mountain separating the towns of
Monroe and *Lyman* was named for him.

Garfield Pond; Mount (4,488 feet)
Franconia, Twin, Willey Ranges

The Haystack is the simple descriptive name this mountain bore
until late in the nineteenth century, and when in the summer of 1871
two Dartmouth graduates, assisting New Hampshire state geologist
Charles H. Hitchcock in his survey of the state, discovered a lake on
the mountain's northwest side they gave the lake the same name, calling it Haystack Lake. But in 1881 President James Garfield was as-

sassinated, and the Franconia selectmen changed the name of The Haystack to honor the slain president. When the name of the peak was changed, the lake's name lost significance, and in 1918 the AMC approved changing the name of the lake to correspond to that of the mountain on which it is located.

Garnet Pools   *Mount Washington, Southern Ridges*

On the *Peabody River* near *Pinkham Notch* are pools in depressions shaped and polished by the abrasive action of water and gravel. The polished appearance of these pools likely accounts for their name.

Gentian Pond   *Mahoosuc Range Area*

This pond and nearby Upper Gentian Pond on the *Appalachian Trail* in the *Mahoosuc Range* were named for gentians, moisture-loving wildflowers widely distributed throughout North America. Though Upper Gentian Pond is the name recognized by GNIS, the AMC calls it Moss Pond.

Georgiana Falls   *Cannon, Kinsman*

As the Bolnicks explain in their *Waterfalls of the White Mountains,* considerable confusion has existed as to the labeling of the two cascades on *Harvard Brook.* The upper fall has been called both Harvard Fall and Harvard Cascade, for its discovery by some Harvard College students prior to 1850, but the Bolnicks, citing authoritative sources, prefer the name Georgiana Falls, labeling it Upper Georgiana Falls to distinguish it from Lower Georgiana Falls 0.5 miles down the stream. The origin of the name Georgiana is unknown.

Giant Falls   *Mahoosuc Range Area*

Located on *Peabody Brook* on *Bald Cap Peak's* southwest slope, these falls were named for their impressive size, though Dream Lake, the source of the water for the falls, is said to be stingy except in the spring.

Giant Stairs   *Mount Washington, Southern Ridges*

To Dr. Samuel Bemis of *Crawford Notch,* two huge steplike ledges between *Mount Resolution* and *Stairs Mountain* suggested giant's stairs, and he proposed the name, as well as the name Stairs Mountain (see entry). The terraces appeared as Giants Stairs on Bond's 1853 map of the White Mountains. A third and similar cliff east of the main summit sometimes is called the Back Stair.

Gibbs Brook, Falls   *Mount Washington, Southern Ridges*

When financial problems blocked Thomas Crawford from completing the hotel he had begun in 1852 at the north end of *Crawford Notch,* he sold the enterprise to Joseph L. Gibb, who finished the hotel later called the Crawford House. His name survives on this brook entering the *Saco River* from the northeast and on the falls 0.4 miles up the brook from Crawford Depot along the *Crawford Path.* Together they are the focus for the WMNF Gibbs Brook Scenic Area.

Gilead   *Mahoosuc Range Area*

In ancient Palestine, Gilead labeled a mountainous region and a city, as well as being a personal name. Early English and American settlers, often deeply religious, were fond of such biblical names— throughout the U.S. mountains were named Pisgah, for the mount from which the Hebrews beheld the Promised Land—and labeling a mountainous region along the *Androscoggin River* in Maine for a mountainous region near the Jordan River in Palestine would have seemed natural and fitting. But the *Dictionary of Maine Place-Names* says the name here comes from the many Balm of Gilead trees in the town's center.

Glen   *Mount Washington, Southern Ridges*

This locality's name, a Gaelic word, simply describes its location in a small valley near the confluence of the *Ellis* and *Saco Rivers.*

The Glen   *North Country*

This tiny community on the north shore of First *Connecticut Lake* has a simple descriptive name taken from Gaelic meaning "small, secluded valley." The name here has been rendered The Glenn, and the locality has been called Stearns Camp, but a 1959 USBGN decision approved the present name.

Glen Boulder Trail *Mount Washington, Southern Ridges*

This path connecting the *Davis Path* with *Glen Ellis Falls* is named for a giant boulder near the lower end of some ledges near timberline. The boulder, which looks as if it is about to roll down the mountain, is so conspicuous that it can be seen from certain points on N.H. Route 16.

Glen Ellis Falls *Mount Washington, Southern Ridges*

These falls on the *Ellis River* were once known as Pitcher Falls, for their shape. Henry Ripley of North Conway, a longtime enthusiast of the White Mountains (see *Ripley Falls*), gave them their present name in 1852, and as such they appeared on Bond's map of 1853.

Tradition says the Indians had a legend about these falls. A daughter of a chief who once ruled this territory loved a youth from a neighboring tribe, but unfortunately her father promised her to one of his own warriors. To resolve the conflict, the father agreed to a bow-drawing contest between the two rivals. The maiden's lover lost. So, defying their people, the two grabbed hands and fled. They were pursued to these falls, where they leaped to their deaths. It is said that sometimes within the mist the shapes of the two lovers can be seen, hand in hand.

Glen House *Mount Washington, Southern Ridges*

Glen is a Gaelic word meaning "small, secluded valley," and that accurately describes the location of this White Mountains landmark in *Pinkham Notch*. The site already was known as The Glen in 1851 when the first Glen House was built, the same year the Atlantic and St. Lawrence Railroad instituted the first passenger service to *Gorham,* and the Glen House quickly became one of the region's most popular resorts. It became even more popular in 1861 with the opening of the carriage road to the summit of *Mount Washington,* with The Glen House at the road's base. But fires have plagued the resort; its buildings were destroyed in 1884, 1893, 1924, and 1967.

Goback Mountain (3,523 feet) *North Country*

According to a journal kept in 1788 by E. W. Judd, this mountain in the town of *Stratford* was named because of its steepness on one side, where all hikers had to "go back."

Goose Eye Mountain, Trail (3,860 feet)

Mahoosuc Range Area

No one knows for sure how this peak in Riley, Maine, got its name. Some persons claim the name is actually Goose High; it is said that geese, in their flights southward from the Rangeley Lakes, fly just high enough to clear the top of this mountain.

Gordon Fall

Northern Peaks, Great Gulf

Like *Gordon Ridge*, this fall on *Snyder Brook* was named for James Gordon of *Gorham*. As the Bolnicks point out in their *Waterfalls of the White Mountains*, "The character of the falls is captured by its old name, *Ripple Falls*, (which appeared in an 1888 *History of Coös County*)." This fall is not to be confused with the Gordon Falls on Gordon Pond Brook in North Woodstock.

Gordon Ridge

Northern Peaks, Great Gulf

James Gordon of *Gorham* guided Rev. Thomas Starr King on the minister's many rambles in the White Mountains; in his book *The White Hills*, Reverend King said Gordon is "as much at home in the woods as a bear." He is said to have cut the first trail up *Mount Madison*; appropriately this northern ridge of the mountain was named for him. See *Gordon Fall*.

Gorham

Mahoosuc Range Area

This town on the *Androscoggin River* originally was part of neighboring *Shelburne*, chartered in 1770; the Gorham area was known as the Shelburne Addition. The town was named Gorham and incorporated in 1836, actions proposed by Sylvester Davis, who was from Gorham, Maine, and a relative of the Gorham family that founded the Maine town. Railroads, which first arrived in 1851, transformed Gorham from a modest farming community into a major rail and tourist center; today logging supplements the sagging rail economy.

Grafton County

The name of this county forming the western border of the White Mountains region comes from Augustus Henry Fitzroy, an English nobleman who espoused the American cause during the pre-Revolutionary era. Among his titles were Earl of Arlington and Euston, Viscount Thetford, Baron Sudbury, and Duke of Grafton.

Fitzroy was related to Gov. Benning Wentworth, who granted and named the town of Grafton in 1761. When his nephew, Gov. John Wentworth, in 1769 designated New Hampshire's original counties, he named all of them for English parliamentarians who supported the American colonies—and those included Duke Fitzroy.

Grafton Notch, Settlement, Township
Mahoosuc Range Area

These features in the northeastern part of the *Mahoosuc Range* in Maine were named by early settler James Brown for Grafton, Massachusetts. Brown passed through the notch in 1830, following a blazed path. Settling above the notch, Brown established a timber business, and by 1838 he had built a mill. The community that grew up around the mill was incorporated as the town of Grafton in 1852. Brown died in 1881.

Grange
North Country

The *Lancaster* Grange Hall, once famous locally for dances held here, gave its name to this tiny settlement east of the village of Lancaster.

Gray Knob
Northern Peaks, Great Gulf

This knob on the northern slopes of *Mount Adams* was named in 1875 by J. Rayner Edmands and William G. Nowell, two noted trail-makers in the White Mountains. The name is doubtless derived from the knob's appearance.

Great Gulf
Northern Peaks, Great Gulf

In colonial times even more than now a "gulf" meant a great chasm or basin, and that exactly describes this huge basin separating *Mount Washington* from the northern peaks of the *Presidential Range.* The Great Gulf originally was called the Gulf of Mexico, for reasons unknown, and it had been observed as early as 1642, when Darby Field, the first non-Indian to climb Mount Washington, reported seeing a huge ravine to the north of the summit. Field did not enter the gulf, and in 1829 Ethan Allen Crawford recounted how he once came to the edge of a "great gulf" while wandering lost in the mountain clouds, but he, too, declined to enter it. The first recorded exploration of the gulf was in 1829 by Dr. J. W. Robbins, a botanist.

Benjamin Willey in 1856 described the gulf as an "almost unfathomable abyss." See Gulfside Trail.

Great Gulf Wilderness Area   *Northern Peaks, Great Gulf*

Designated by the USFS in 1964 to include 5,552 acres of the *Great Gulf*.

Greeley Brook, Ledges, Ponds   *Waterville Valley*

These features near *Waterville Valley* undoubtedly were named for Nathaniel Greeley, who settled in Waterville Valley around 1830 and prospered despite great obstacles. He acquired farmlands, built two hotels—one of which burned—and was generally well-liked and respected in the region. The ponds west of *Mount Kancamagus* are now the focus for the WMNF Greeley Ponds Scenic Area. The ledges, sometimes labeled simply The Ledges, are northeast of the village of Waterville Valley.

Green Hills   *Carter, Baldface Ranges*

These low, forested hills east of North Conway bear a common name describing the color of their vegetation, a name reminiscent of the Green Mountains of Vermont. Ironically, the highest summit of the Green Hills is 2,370-foot *Black Cap*.

Greens Grant   *Mount Washington, Southern Ridges*

This unincorporated tract of land adjacent to *Mount Washington* just north of the *Glen House* was one of the last grants made by Gov. John Wentworth to soldiers of the French and Indian Wars before the Revolutionary War broke out. He made the grant to Lt. Francis Green of Boston.

Groveton   *North Country*

A large grove of maple trees once stood where the Groveton railroad station is now. It is reported that, when the trees were cut down, the village was named Grove Town, later elided to Groveton. Groveton is in the town of *Northumberland*.

Gulf of Slides

Mount Washington, Southern Ridges

Countless landslides have scarred the upper slopes of the broad ravine southeast of *Boott Spur,* and from these slides the ravine got its name.

Gulfside Trail

Northern Peaks, Great Gulf

This trail leading from *Madison* Hut to the summit of *Mount Washington* was named by J. Rayner Edmands (see *Edmands Col*), who, starting in 1892, located and constructed most of the trail, often using cairns to mark the route. He named it because the trail traverses the side of the *Great Gulf.*

Guyot, Mount (4,589 feet)

Franconia, Twin, Willey Ranges

Prof. Arnold Guyot—pronounced GHEE-yoh—(1807–84) of Princeton was a physical geographer who wrote learned papers about the *Appalachian Mountains.* Guyot visited the White Mountains often, and in 1857 he made the first ascent of *Mount Carrigain.* In 1860 he published a small but good map of the White Mountains, supplanting the previous best map of the region, that by Prof. G. P. Bond of Harvard. Guyot named many features in the White Mountains, including *Mount Tripyramid,* and in 1851 he estimated *Mount Washington's* elevation at 6,291 feet, only three feet off the current estimate. But Guyot's interest in mountains went far beyond the White Mountains. It was Guyot who determined that Clingmans Dome was the highest point of the Smokies and not Mount Buckley. (He also proved that Mount Washington was not the highest summit in the eastern U.S.; it is Mount Mitchell, 6,684 feet, in North Carolina.) And, by choosing *On the Appalachian Mountain System* as the title for his great geological treatise, he helped establish that the name of the range would be Appalachian and not Allegheny, a matter not previously settled (see *Appalachian Mountains*). In 1876 the AMC named this peak north of *Mount Bond* in the *Twin Mountain* Range for him. A 13,370-foot mountain in the Colorado Rockies, a 6,621-foot summit in the Smokies, and a 12,305-foot peak in Sequoia National Park in California—and even a crater on the moon—also commemorate this pioneer geographer.

Hadleys Purchase
Mount Washington, Southern Ridges

In 1834 Henry G. Hadley of Eugene City, Oregon, paid $500 to Commissioner James Willey and received one of the hitherto unassigned tracts of land in the White Mountains. Hadley's Purchase consisted of slightly more than 8,000 acres, a narrow mountainous strip of land above *Crawford Notch* and east of *Harts Location*.

Hale Brook; Mount (4,077 feet)
Franconia, Twin, Willey Ranges

New Hampshire state geologist Charles H. Hitchcock in 1874 named this peak in the *Twin Mountain* Range for Rev. Edward Everett Hale (1822–1909). Reverend Hale came from a well-known Boston family, and in addition to being associated with civic improvement and philanthropic work in Boston he also was an author, whose short story "The Man Without a Country" has become an American classic. In 1841 Hale was appointed a member of the State Geological Survey, and, according to Hitchcock, Reverend Hale "assisted Dr. [Charles T.] Jackson in exploring the White Mountains, and has done much to make them famous through his writings." Reverend Hale also was a member of the Society for the Protection of New Hampshire Forests (SPNHF); when the Society was organized in 1901, Reverend Hale called the meeting at *Intervale* to open the campaign for the National White Mountain Forest Reserve. See also *Lend-a-Hand Trail*.

Hales Location
Carrigain, Moat Regions

This 1,215-acre tract bordering *Echo Lake* near North Conway was granted in 1771 to Samuel Hale of Portsmouth, a major in the

New Hampshire Provincial Army. Major Hale lived in Portsmouth until his death in 1807, and no settlement of his location ever was made, though his heirs maintained residences in *Conway* to oversee the grant. The land is now part of the WMNF.

Halls Ledge   *Carter, Baldface Ranges*

The best conjecture is that this outlook near N.H. Route 16 in *Jackson* is named for Joseph S. Hall, a *Lancaster* resident who helped explore *Tuckerman Ravine* in 1852. As a contractor, Hall was among those persons responsible for the first summit house on *Mount Washington* and for the carriage road.

Halls Stream   *North Country*

In 1776 an army of American soldiers entered the wilderness of northern New Hampshire in a bold move to invade Quebec. It was a harsh and perilous journey; the soldiers became demoralized, hungry, and exhausted as they traveled; desertion was rife among the troops. According to one account, one deserter was named Hall, who left the army in Quebec and dragged himself as far as a creek known locally as Clear Stream. There he knelt to drink, but he was so weak from hunger and exhaustion that he could not raise his head again and drowned.

Another version of the story says Hall was not a deserter at all but had been left at Clear Stream by his comrades because he was too weak to continue. When the soldiers returned they found him dead by the stream; they buried him here. Halls Stream today forms part the New Hampshire-Quebec border.

Hammond Trail   *Chocorua, East Sandwich*

In its *Bicentennial Observance,* the Town of Albany noted that this, the oldest trail up *Mount Chocorua,* was built by and named for one of the ancestors of Mrs. Ina Morrill, who as of 1966 was *Albany* town tax collector. The trail begins at the old Hammond Farm.

Hancock Notch; Mount (4,403 feet)
Carrigain, Moat Regions

Mount Hancock, west of *Mount Carrigain,* originally was called Pemigewasset Peak for its proximity to the *Pemigewasset River* to the south, but it later was renamed to honor John Hancock, the first signer of the Declaration of Independence.

The mountain is a long ridge, with its principal summits North Peak, 4,403 feet, and South Peak, 4,274 feet. Hancock Notch is south of the peaks.

Hark Hill (1,118 feet)   *Mahoosuc Range Area*

Legend says some settlers living on the *Androscoggin River* once fled to this hill to hide from raiding Indians. They spent the night on the hill, keeping watchful silence, and the next day they made their escape. As they "harked" for signs of danger, the legend says, the name of the hill was born. While this apocryphal explanation clearly smacks of folk-etymology, no other explanation is known.

Hart Ledge   *Mount Washington, Southern Ridges*

Col. John Hart, as a reward for service in the French and Indian Wars, was granted lands near the *Saco River* west of *Bartlett,* and this cliff above the bend in the river here was named for him. See *Harts Location.*

Harts Location   *Franconia, Twin, Willey Ranges*

Harts Location in *Crawford Notch* is among the most historic sites in the White Mountains. It was here that occurred the avalanche that wiped out the Willey family (see *Mount Willey*), and it was here that lived Dr. Samuel Bemis, called "Lord of the Valley." Abel Crawford is buried here. The name Harts Location is derived from Col. John Hart of Portsmouth, to whom Gov. John Wentworth granted these lands as a reward for service in the French and Indian Wars. The region originally had been called the Notch of the White Hills. See *Harts Ledge.*

Harvard Brook, Falls   *Cannon, Kinsman*

These features on a branch of the *Pemigewasset River* were named for their discovery by a group of Harvard College students sometime prior to 1850. See *Georgiana Falls.*

Hastings Campground; Mount (2,167 feet)
Carter, Baldface Ranges

In the 1880s, Maj. Gideon Hastings commenced timber operations on *Evans Brook,* and soon the company settlement of Hastings
sprang up. Large mills were fed timber from the Wild River valley,
transported over a logging railroad. Today, Major Hastings's timber
holdings are within the WMNF, and the village of Hastings has vanished, but its existence is recalled by the Hastings Campground, near
the village's site near the confluence of *Wild River* and Evans Brook,
and by Mount Hastings to the southwest.

Haverhill
Connecticut Region

Most settlers of this town on the *Connecticut River* were from
Haverhill, Massachusetts, and they named their new home for their
old one. Haverhill, New Hampshire, includes the broad floodplain
through which the Connecticut meanders, and the region was originally called the Lower Cohoss, from an Abenaki word meaning
"pines."

Hawthorne Brook, Falls
Franconia, Twin, Willey Ranges

Nature is a frequent theme in the work of Nathaniel Hawthorne,
the nineteenth-century American writer, and this sentiment would
have been nurtured by his visits to the White Mountains. His short
story "The Great Stone Face" made the profile in *Franconia Notch*
famous. This brook draining the col immediately east of *Mount Garfield* was named for him, as is an obscure but charming waterfall in
a ravine off the *Gale River* Trail.

Hayes, Mount (2,566 feet)
Mahoosuc Range Area

Mrs. Margaret Hayes was the first proprietor of the White Mountains Station House in *Gorham,* later called the Alpine House, built
in 1851 by the Grand Trunk Railroad. Born in Portsmouth in 1804
and later married to Col. Charles Hayes of Bangor, Maine, she was
widowed in 1839. In 1851 she entered into co-ownership with N. C.
Woodward of The White Mountains Station House; her biographer
described her as "a lady of great energy of character who acquired a
deserved popularity for her successful management of the hotel."
This mountain in Gorham was named for her—Rev. Thomas Starr
King called it "her monument"—and it appeared as Mount Hayes
on Franklin Leavitt's 1852 map of the White Mountains."

Haystack (general)

"Haystack" always has been a common metaphor describing mountains. In the White Mountains are several, listed below.

In addition, several other peaks now bearing other names earlier had been called Haystack. *Mount Garfield* was called The Haystack; *Mount Lafayette* was called the Great Haystack; while the smaller summits nearby, *Liberty* and *Flume,* were called simply the Haystacks. Also, *Mounts Tripyramid, Osceola, Tecumseh, Black, Sandwich,* and *Jennings* once were known as the Waterville Haystacks. See *Bartlett Haystack.*

Haystack (2,060 feet)   *Carrigain, Moat Regions*

Summit southwest of North Conway, south of *South Moat.*

Haystack Lake   *Franconia, Twin, Willey Ranges*

See *Garfield Pond; Mount.*

Haystack Mountain (2,713 feet)
Franconia, Twin, Willey Ranges

Prominent rocky peak, also sometimes called The Nubble, at the lower end of *North Twin's* north ridge.

Haystack Mountain (approx. 2,100 feet)
Speckled Mountain Region

This small summit is better known for the name it gave to Haystack Notch and the Haystack Notch Trail, connecting Maine Route 113 with the *Miles Notch* Trail.

Heermance Camp   *Chocorua, East Sandwich*

This camp in a sheltered hollow near the summit of *Mount Whiteface* was built in 1912 and named in honor of Rev. Edgar L. Heermance, who has been described as "one of those enthusiastic mountaineering ministers to which the mountains of this whole section owe so much of their history and popularity." Reverend Heermance spent summers in *Chocorua.*

Hellgate

This point on the *Diamond River* was named during the logging era, when river drivers had a hellish time getting their logs through the constricted channel without jamming.

Hemenway State Forest

It was from the Tamworth estate of Augustus Hemenway that this state forest was created in 1932; its name preserves his memory.

Hermit Lake

In 1853 S. B. Beckett of Portland, Maine, published a guide to the White Mountains, and this tiny lake at the foot of *Tuckerman Ravine* was named by him, for reasons unknown.

Hibbard Mountain (3,200 feet)

In the *Wonalancet* Range southeast of *Mount Passaconaway* is this peak named in honor of Judge E. A. Hibbard of Laconia.

Hight, Mount (4,690 feet)

An early settler named Hight gave his name to this peak adjacent to *Carter Dome*. Dr. Jeremy Belknap's *Journal* of 1792 mentions a Mr. Hight living on Colonel Whipple's estate in *Jefferson,* and it is reported that Hight was a companion of Prof. Ezra Carter on the professor's many explorations in the White Mountains. Moses F. Sweetser, in his guide, told an apocryphal story of two hunters, named Carter and Hight, who having become separated climbed the mountains near them, Carter ascending what is now Carter Dome, Hight climbing what is now *Wildcat Mountain*. The mountains for several years bore the two hunters' names, but when Prof. Arnold Guyot gave Wildcat Mountain its name, Hight's name was placed on another peak. It is possible the Hight in all these accounts was the same man, and the accounts are not mutually exclusive, but the specific circumstances of the naming likely will never be known.

Hincks Trail

E. J. Hincks cut this trail connecting the Spur Trail and *Randolph Path* with *Gray Knob* on *Nowell Ridge*.

Hitchcock Fall, Mountain (2,804 feet)

Franconia, Twin, Willey Ranges

Few persons have been more responsible for the exploration and naming of the White Mountains' geologic features than Prof. Charles H. Hitchcock. The son of a noted geologist, he became a geologist himself, and in 1868 he was named state geologist of New Hampshire. In that capacity he conducted a detailed geological survey of the state, and his three-volume *Geology of New Hampshire,* which included an atlas, still is an outstanding reference. He also was professor of geology and mineralogy at Dartmouth College, a position he held for forty years.

Professor Hitchcock was a tireless and enthusiastic explorer of the White Mountains, and he named many previously unnamed features. In recognition, perhaps, a mountain and two waterfalls were named for him. The fall on *Mount Willard* was discovered by Professor Hitchcock and Prof. J. D. Dana while they were exploring in 1875 for the state geological survey, and was subsequently named for Professor Hitchcock. A fall on *Bumpus Brook* north of *Mount Madison* also possibly was named for him. And in 1877 Warren Upham honored him by giving his name to a spur of *Mount Field.*

Hitchcock Fall

Northern Peaks, Great Gulf

Two men named Hitchcock might have given their name to this fall on *Bumpus Brook.* One was New Hampshire state geologist Charles H. Hitchcock (see *Mount Hitchcock*). The other was Col. John R. Hitchcock, who managed not only the Alpine House in *Gorham* but also the *Tip Top House* on the summit of *Mount Washington* and a lodge on the summit of *Mount Moriah,* as well as being a director of the Mount Washington Carriage Road Company. The two Hitchcocks were contemporaries; exactly which inspired this name is unknown.

Hogback (general)

"Hogback" is a common descriptive metaphor for a ridge of upwardly tilted sedimentary rocks. In the White Mountains the name appears in *Waterville Valley* and northeast of East *Haverhill.*

The Horn (3,903 feet)

North Country

A small but prominent outcrop rising hornlike above the forest in the *Pilot Range,* one mile northeast of *Mount Cabot.*

Horne Brook   *Mahoosuc Range Area*

This brook flowing into the *Androscoggin River* above *Berlin Falls* also has been known as Mollywocket Brook (see *Molly Ocket*), though a 1972 USBGN descision established the present name. The origin of the name Horne Brook is unknown, but a possible explanation is that it is related to nearby *Leavitt Brook*.

Howker Ridge   *Northern Peaks, Great Gulf*

James Howker had a farm in *Randolph* near the foot of this ridge leading to the summit of *Mount Madison*. On the ridge are four rocky knobs that have come to be called the Howks. The Howker Ridge Trail was cut by Charles Torrey, a professor of semitic languages at Yale and among the early trailmakers who spent summers in Randolph.

Huntington, Mount (3,670 feet)   *Carrigain, Moat Regions*

In 1877, Warren Upham named this peak south of *Hancock Notch* for assistant state geologist J. H. Huntington; see *Huntington Ravine*.

Huntington Ravine   *Mount Washington, Southern Ridges*

In 1870–71 a party led by assistant state geologist J. H. Huntington of Hanover spent a winter on *Mount Washington,* a mountain said with little contradiction to have the world's worst weather outside Alaska and Antarctica. (Huntington prepared for this by spending the winter of 1869–70 atop *Mount Moosilauke.*) The Mount Washington project was so successful that in 1871 the U.S. Signal Service set up a weather observatory on the summit. For this feat, Huntington's associates named this huge cirque on Mount Washington's east side for him. In the time of Rev. Thomas Starr King, about ten years earlier, the ravine had been called appropriately the Grand Gulf, not to be confused with the *Great Gulf* on the mountain's northern side. In a letter, William Oakes, the botanist, explorer, and writer about the White Mountains, referred to the cirque as "dark ravine," though this reference could have been merely descriptive.

Hurricane Mountain (2,101 feet)   *Carter, Baldface Ranges*

Presumably a hurricane had something to do with the naming of this peak midway between *Intervale* and South *Chatham,* but the exact circumstances have been lost. The peak previously was called Green Mountain.

Hutchins Mountain (3,710 feet)   *North Country*

See *Mount Pilot.*

I

Ice Gulch
Ice Gulch *North Country*

Ice Gulch   *North Country*   75

On the southeast slope of the *Crescent Range* in *Randolph* is a long, deep gouge in the earth, and in the trough are boulder caves that receive very little sunlight and hence remain cool and damp even in summer. Ice can be found in the caves all year long.

Imp Mountain (3,708 feet)
Imp Profile (3,165 feet) *Carter, Baldface Ranges*

A resemblance to a distorted human profile gave Imp Profile, also known as Imp Face, its name. The cliff, a west spur of *North Carter*, is best seen from the *Dolly Copp* Road at the monument marking the site of the Dolly Copp house, and it is said that Dolly Copp herself gave the mountain its name. Imp Brook heads on this mountain's south slope and runs west into the *Peabody River*. Imp Mountain is 1.5 miles northeast of Imp Face; the Imp Shelter is on its northeast slope.

Indian Head *Cannon, Kinsman*

See *Mount Pemigewasset*.

Indian Leap *Moosilauke Region*

Every region, it seems, has a cliff called Indian Leap, named usually for an apocryphal legend involving an Indian maiden and her lover. But the legend—not involving a love story—behind the cliffs two miles east of North *Woodstock* is more credible than most. It says that when the time came for an Indian boy to prove his manhood he was taken to this spot on *Moosilauke Brook* where he had to leap a 5.5-foot span, with a plunge down a cliff the price to be paid for unsteady nerves. The waterfall here also is known as Agassiz Basin, for the great Swiss naturalist, Jean Louis Rudolph Agassiz (see *Mount Agassiz*).

Indian Stream   *North Country*

This name is unique among White Mountains place names in that it also was once the name of an independent nation. That, at least, is how the settlers along this stream near the Canadian border viewed their region in 1832. Disgruntled by the U.S. and Canada squabbling over which nation owned the land, they tried to settle the issue by seceding from both. They formed an independent nation called the Indian Stream Republic, and they promptly set about creating their own stamps, currency, government, and other appurtenances of a sovereign realm. Their little experiment lasted only a few years, and by the Treaty of Washington in 1842 the region had become a permanent part of the U.S.

The name Indian Stream comes from Indians remaining in this region longer than they survived elsewhere in New Hampshire. Before Indian Stream became the accepted name, the region was known as Wales Location for one Nathaniel Wales; it also was known as Liberty and Bedels and Others Grant.

Ingalls, Mount (2,253 feet)   *Mahoosuc Range Area*

This peak was named for the Ingalls family (see *Moses Rock*), pioneer settlers of *Shelburne*; Daniel Ingalls and other family members arrived 1770–72. A 1936 USBGN decision established Mount Ingalls as the accepted form and not Ingalls Mountain. Another decision that year affixed the name to this peak and not to the peak now known as *Mount Success*.

Inlook Trail   *Northern Peaks, Great Gulf*

This trail from the *Randolph Path* to the Kelton Trail was named for several "inlooks" up the *Snyder Brook* valley to *Mounts Adams* and *John Quincy Adams*.

Intervale   *Carter, Baldface Ranges*

An intervale is a level opening in a river valley, and this village north of North Conway was named for being on a shelf above the great intervale on the *Saco River.* The intervale once was known locally as Fosters Pocket (see *Conway*).

Iron Bluff, Mountain (2,716 feet)
Mount Washington, Southern Ridges

When iron mines were opened on this mountain west of *Jackson,* the name was changed from Baldface to Iron Mountain. Iron Bluff at the end of the Iron Mountain's easterly spur had been called Ducks Head, for its shape as seen from nearby pastures, but on June 11, 1915, the AMC Committee on Nomenclature recommended Iron Bluff as the preferred name.

Isolation, Mount (4,005 feet)
Mount Washington, Southern Ridges

Located near *Montalban Ridge*'s northern edge, this peak was named by the White Mountains explorer Prof. William H. Pickering, doubtless because the mountain is indeed isolated.

Israel Ridge *Northern Peaks, Great Gulf*

This northeast ridge of *Mount Jefferson* was named around 1891 by J. Rayner Edmands, most likely because the *Israel River* heads near here. Before that the ridge had been called Emerald Tongue, a name suggested by Miss Marian M. Pychowska. (See also entry for *Edmands.*)

Israel River *Northern Peaks, Great Gulf*

Indians called this small but vigorous river in *Jefferson* and *Lancaster* by a name variously transliterated "Siwoog-a-nock" and "Singrawac," variously translated as "a place where we return in the springtime" and "foaming stream with white rock." Sometime prior to 1750 Israel Glines and his brother, John, visited the region to hunt and trap, and Israel set up his camp on the river that today bears his name. (John camped near what is now *Johns River* in *Whitefield.*) In 1754 another party visited the region, and they named the river for Capt. Peter Powers, a leader of the party who wrote about the river in his journal, but the new name didn't stick. The river sometimes is called Israels River, but this variant never has had official acceptance.

Jackman Brook   *Moosilauke Region*

This brook heads southwest of North Woodstock and flows northeast to form *Moosilauke Brook*. Jackman was a common name among the region's early settlers, and two brothers—Lyman and Royal—with that surname were among the "finders" of *Lost River,* a short distance to the north.

Jackman Falls   *Cannon, Kinsman*

These falls in *Kinsman Notch* are at the site of the old Jackman Mill. Jackman was a common name among the region's early settlers.

Jackson   *Carter, Baldface Ranges*

The first settlers of this town called it New Madbury because most of them were from the New Hampshire seacoast town of Madbury. In 1800 the town was incorporated under the name of Adams, to honor President John Adams, then in office. But the town liked John Adams better than it liked his son, John Quincy Adams, and in 1828, during the presidential race between John Quincy Adams and Andrew Jackson, all the voters in the town except one went with the nationwide majority and voted for Jackson. Soon after, and with the blessings of Gov. Benjamin Pierce, a staunch Democrat and supporter of Jackson, the name was changed to honor the seventh president of the U.S. instead of the second.

Jackson, Mount (4,052 feet)
Mount Washington, Southern Ridges

In 1848 the exploring botanists William Oakes and Frederick Huntington built a fire on the south spur of *Mount Pierce* and named the spur *Mount Jackson*. Some persons say the peak was named to honor President Andrew Jackson, but records of the AMC say it was to honor Dr. Charles T. Jackson, New Hampshire state geologist, who himself was responsible for the naming of White Mountains features such as *Mount Hale.*

Jackson Falls   *Carter, Baldface Ranges*

This series of cataracts and pools on *Wildcat River* takes its name from the village of *Jackson,* just to the southwest.

Jefferson   *North Country*

The town's first name was Dartmouth, after William Legge, second Earl of Dartmouth, who was the English patron of Dartmouth College and a friend of the American colonies. In 1765, after the end of the Seven Years War, the town was granted to several persons, and among the early settlers was Col. Joseph Whipple of Portsmouth, a wealthy merchant and shipowner who cut the first path through the forests to build his famous "manor." Colonel Whipple was an enthusiastic Jeffersonian Democrat, and his brother and partner, William Whipple, was one of New Hampshire's three signers of the Declaration of Independence, a document written by Jefferson. It was through Colonel Whipple's efforts and influence that the name Dartmouth was changed to Jefferson—four years *before* Jefferson became president. The village of Jefferson, on the south slope of *Mount Starr King,* sometimes is known locally as Jefferson Hill, while the community at the south base of *Boy Mountain* is called Jefferson Highlands.

Jefferson Notch; Mount (5,715 feet)
Northern Peaks, Great Gulf

The third highest peak in the White Mountains was named by the Weeks-Brackett party (see *Presidential Range*), receiving its name when most of the other peaks of the Presidential Range did. Jeffersons Knees, the peak's truncated eastern ridges, and Jefferson Ravine were named by the early botanist and explorer William H. Pickering. Jefferson Notch on the west, separating Mount Jefferson from the *Dartmouth Range,* was named in 1899 by John Anderson of the Mount Washington Hotel at *Bretton Woods.*

Jennings Peak (3,500 feet) *Waterville Valley Region*

This peak near *Sandwich Mountain* was named for "Captivity" Jennings, the baby girl carried off by Indians to Canada, from whence she eventually was ransomed. The peak also has been known as Dennisons Peak, likely for an early settler.

Jericho Mountain (2,487 feet) *North Country*

The origin of the name of this peak west of *Berlin* is unknown. It originally was called Black Mountain.

Jewell Trail *Northern Peaks, Great Gulf*

Leading from the Base Road parking area to the *Gulfside Trail,* the Jewell Trail commemorates Sgt. W. S. Jewell, a U.S. Army Signal Corps observer on *Mount Washington* 1878–80, who died in 1884 while a member of the Greeley expedition to the Arctic.

Jigger Johnson Campground *Waterville Valley Region*

Albert Lewis "Jigger" Johnson was an almost legendary North Country woods boss during the region's colorful logging era. For sixty-four years he was a logger, river driver, and camp boss. Later he became a forest fire lookout on *Mount Chocorua* and *Carter Dome,* spending much time improving trails there. This WMNF campground on the *Kancamagus Highway* preserves his memory.

Jim Liberty Shelter *Chocorua, East Sandwich*

James Liberty was an enterprising Frenchman who lived most of his life in the White Mountains. In 1887 he and some other local residents improved an old trail up *Mount Chocorua*—now called the Liberty Trail—and charged a twenty-five cent toll. They built a stone camp beneath the peak, but high winds blew off the canvas roof, and timber for another roof had burned, so they set up a bunch of tents inside the stone walls. When the tents were full, "lodgekeeper" Liberty slept under the sky on a bed of hemlock boughs. He would signal his presence at the camp by lighting a fire that could be seen from the valley below, and he would welcome guests by brewing them some strong green tea and singing strange French songs while he played the accordion and puffed an old clay pipe. In 1892 David Knowles built a two-story hotel known as the Peak House, which stood until it was felled by high winds in 1915. The stone stable was rebuilt by the Chocorua Mountain Club in 1924 and named the Jim Liberty Shelter. In 1932 strong winds again damaged the structure, but it was replaced in 1934 by the USFS.

Jobildunc Ravine   *Moosilauke Region*

It is commonly supposed that the name of this ravine between *Mount Moosilauke* and *Mount Blue* is of Indian origin. But in North Woodstock there is a tradition that says the ravine is an amalgam of the first names of three hikers who explored it—Joe, Bill, and Duncan.

Johnson   *Cannon, Kinsman*

This was an ephemeral timber company town, organized in 1904 around a sawmill and logging operations established by George L. Johnson, who also built the Gordon Pond Railroad to the site in order to haul logs from *Kinsman Mountain*. In 1916 the railroad ceased running, and the settlement died soon after.

Johns River   *Connecticut Region*

This river in *Whitefield,* like the *Israel River* in *Lancaster* and *Jefferson,* was named for one of the Glines brothers, John and Israel. They visited the area sometime before 1740, and each set up a hunting-trapping camp on the river named for him. In 1754 an exploring party passing through the region heard the name and, knowing nothing of John Glines, thought the river was named for Ensign John Stark, who had been captured by Indians while hunting near the Johns River mouth. This same John Stark later became the Revolutionary War general who was a hero at the battles of Bennington and Bunker Hill.

Jordan Brook, Mountain (2,653 feet)
Mahoosuc Range Area

Benjamin Jordan was a settler here by 1843. The brook heads on the small summit and flows north to the *Sunday River.*

Joseph Story Reservation   *Cannon, Kinsman*

This 150-acre tract of forest land near North Woodstock and *Lincoln* was given to the AMC in 1897 by Miss Sarah B. Fay in memory of her father, whose name it bears.

Josh Billings Spring   *Mount Washington, Southern Ridges*

Josh Billings (1818–85) was a noted American humorist and lecturer; he liked to fish in the brooks near this spring in *Pinkham Notch*.

Kancamagus, Mount (3,728 feet) *Waterville Valley Region*

This mass of rounded ridges between *Mounts Tripyramid, Huntington,* and *Osceola* was named in 1876 by New Hampshire state geologist Charles H. Hitchcock for the seventeenth-century Penacook leader, Kancamagus. He is said to have wanted to be a friend to the English, but he was abused and mistreated, and finally he led the Penacooks in their last uprising against the white settlers, the 1686 raid on Dover. Then, defeated and disheartened, he and his people retreated to the village of St. Francis, Quebec. Kancamagus was the nephew of the Penacook chief Wonalancet (see *Wonalancet*) and the grandson of Chief Passaconaway (see *Passaconaway*); the place names of the White Mountains are all that recall their presence here.

Kancamagus Highway, Pass *Waterville Valley Region*

The highway and its highest point, Kancamagus Pass, were named for nearby Mount Kancamagus, named in turn for the seventeenth-century Penacook leader Kancamagus (see *Mount Kancamagus*). The route began in 1837 with a town road laid out along the *Swift River* to *Passaconaway*. In the mid-1920s a single-lane gravel road was begun. Other improvements followed until the final 1.2-mile section connecting Passaconaway and *Lincoln* was completed in 1959, though it wasn't completely paved until 1964. In 1989 the USFS designated the route a National Scenic Byway.

Katherine, Mount (1,910 feet) *Chocorua, East Sandwich*

West of *Wonalancet*; see *Sleeper Ridge*.

Kearsarge North, Mount (3,268 feet)

Carter, Baldface Ranges

Considerable discussion and controversy has focused on this pyramid-shaped peak north of *Conway*. Not only is the origin of the name Kearsarge complex and obscure, but also the name is duplicated on another New Hampshire mountain, in the town of Warner in Merrimack County, a situation that has nettled generations of geographers and historians.

At least part of the difficulty results from the peak having had a dual identity over the years. It appeared on Thomas Jeffries's 1774 map as the Pigwakket Hills, this name clearly coming from Pequawket, the Indian village at the site of what is now Conway. But Dr. Jeremy Belknap's map of 1791 showed the mountains as Kyarsarge, and it has been suggested that Dr. Belknap took the name from a still earlier map. John Farmer and Jacob B. Monroe, in their 1823 Gazetteer of the State of New Hampshire, referred to the mountains as Piquawket. Rev. Thomas Starr King, writing in the 1850s, believed the mountain's original name was *Pequaket,* though he personally advocated changing the name of the "queenly mountain" to Martha Washington.

Yet, during and despite all this, local inhabitants of the Conway region were calling the mountain Kiarsarge, and when the old Pequawket Indian Sabatis was asked the peak's Indian name, he replied "Ke-sough" or "Ke-a-sock," Indian pronunciations not easily fitted to English spellings.

The smoldering confusion and contention about the name were fanned by the existence of the other Mount Kearsarge in Warner, and in 1876 it was proposed to change the name of the northern peak. The move failed, but not before Conway residents became very vocal over the issue. At the time the Conway judge Joel Eastman wrote: "All, from the oldest to the youngest, still call the mountain Kiarsarge, throughout this oldest section of the country, and any attempt to change the name will be futile. It will still go by the name of Kiarsarge until the Day of Judgment, and afterwards, if the memory of things of this world remain after that day. . . ."

It is too early to tell about Judgment Day, but so far Judge Eastman was correct about the durability of the name Kearsarge. Although the USBGN in 1915 officially adopted the name Pequawket, it continued to be called Kearsarge, and finally in 1959 the USBGN overturned its earlier decision and pronounced that the northern peak be called Kearsarge North.

But from whence came the name Kearsarge?

An Indian origin is most likely. It not known what Sabatis said the name meant to him, and without his authority we're left with numerous other translations. One is that the name comes from "kesarzet," an Abenaki word meaning "the proud, selfish," and the peak does indeed stand aloof and alone. Kearsarge can also be translated into Abenaki to mean "pointed mountain, high place," as well as "land that is harsh, rough, difficult," all also valid descriptions. Another Abenaki word the name has been thought to be derived from is "Cowischewaschook," a title the Abenakis are supposed to have applied to the mountain, meaning "notched and pointed mountain of pines." Other persons have said the name is simply a euphonization of two Abenaki descriptive words, "kees" meaning "high," and "-auke," a suffix meaning "place." And the *History of Carroll County* says the name doesn't come from Abenaki at all but from "ke-sough," an Algonquian word meaning "born of the hill that first shakes hands with the morning light."

Any—or none—of these explanations might be correct.

Kedron Brook   *Franconia, Twin, Willey Ranges*

This short stream heads on *Mount Willey*'s southeast slope and runs south and east to join the *Saco River* in *Crawford Notch*. The name comes from the Bible, where Kedron is a stream in Israel rising on the east side of Jerusalem and separating it from the Mount of Olives, eventually flowing into the Dead Sea. Several features in the White Mountains have such biblical names.

Kenduskeag Trail   *Cater, Baldface Ranges*

Kenduskeag is said to approximate an Abenaki Indian word meaning "a pleasant walk," a delightful name for a mountain trail. This connects the Carter-Moriah Trail with the Shelburne Trail.

Kidderville   *North Country*

Around 1830 a man named Moody Little built a sawmill near the site of this hamlet east of *Colebrook*. Soon after, the sawmill was purchased and refitted by Abial Kidder, and the little settlement has borne his name ever since.

Kilkenny   *North Country*

County Kilkenny in eastern Ireland shares its name with this un-incorporated, uninhabited town containing *Mount Cabot*, the highest summit north of the *Presidential Range.* The town was not always uninhabited, but in the 1820s the writer John Farmer described Kilkenny as having "very few inhabitants and they are very poor and for aught that appears to the contrary they must remain so as they may be deemed actually trespassers on that part of God's heritage which he designed for the reservation of bears, wolves, moose, and other animals of the forest." Between 1887 and 1897 the Lancaster and Kilkenny Railway Company operated a logging line into the area—cross-country skiers use the old railroad bed—but despite that nothing much has happened in Kilkenny to alter Farmer's assessment.

Kilkenny Ridge Trail   *North Country*

A recent USFS trail traversing the mountainous north-south ridge in the town of *Kilkenny.*

Kimball Brook   *North Country*

George Kimball came to the town of *Stratford* around 1812; this small brook flowed through his farm.

Kimball Ponds   *Cater, Baldface Ranges*

The origin of the name of these ponds northeast of South Chatham is unknown, but they first appeared on Samuel Holland's 1784 map as Kimballs Ponds. *Upper Kimball Pond,* slightly south of *Lower Kimball Pond,* ironically appears lower on the map than its neighbor. Upper Kimball Pond has been called Kimball Lake and also Webb Pond, but the present name was established by the USBGN in 1980.

Kineo, Mount (3,320 feet)   *Moosilauke Region*

In Abenaki *kineo* means "sharp peak," hence the name of this peak east of Warren.

King Ravine; King Ravine Trail   *Northern Peaks, Great Gulf*

Rev. Thomas Starr King, the White Mountains explorer and publicist, in 1857 led the first party to explore this huge cirque on the north side of *Mount Adams.* In his 1859 book, *The White Hills: Their Legends, Landscapes, and Poetry,* Reverend King called the huge bowl Adams Ravine, but it later came to bear his own name instead; see *Mount Starr King.* The King Ravine Trail, connecting

Lowes Path to *Air Line* via King Ravine, was built by Charles E. Lowe in 1876. Along this trail is a well-known section fancifully called the Subway, because it goes beneath huge boulders and through boulder caves; an alternative route is called the Elevated.

Kinsman Mountain *Cannon, Kinsman*

Asa Kinsman and his wife arrived in the town of *Easton* in the 1780s with all their belongings piled on a two-wheeled cart pulled by a yoke of oxen, and they literally had to hew their way through the wilderness to take up their claim. Kinsman is buried in a little cemetery in Easton. The ridge known as Kinsman Mountain is dominated by 4,358-foot South Peak, sometimes known as South Kinsman; it appears in GNIS by its full but unwieldy title South Peak Kinsman Mountain. GNIS lists the northern summit, just southwest of Kinsman Pond, as North Peak, 4,293 feet, though it appears in some guides as North Kinsman. The height-of-land between South Kinsman and Mount Wolf to the south has been known as Kinsman Notch.

Ladd Pond
North Country

Daniel Ladd settled near this pond in *Stewartstown* and gave his name to it. The pond was known for the loup-cervier, or Canadian lynx, that frequented it, and Ladd and his son David set about exterminating them, partly to be rid of them and partly for the bounty.

Lafayette, Mount (5,249 feet)
Franconia, Twin, Willey Ranges

This peak east of *Franconia Notch* originally was called the Great Haystack by early settlers because of its shape—it appeared thus on Philip Carrigain's map of 1816—and the smaller peaks nearby—*Liberty* and *Flume*—were simply called the Haystacks; see *Haystack (general)*. Rev. Timothy Dwight (1752–1817), president of Yale University, who led two trips to the mountain, once proposed naming the mountain Wentworth after New Hampshire's last colonial governor, John Wentworth, but nothing came of his idea.

The mountain received its present name as a way of honoring the visit to America in 1824–25 of the French nobleman the Marquis de Lafayette, who aided the American colonists during the Revolutionary War. In 1826 the following letter signed by "R. S." appeared in the Boston *Courier*: "On the last anniversary of the Battle of Yorktown, a respectable assemblage of the citizens of Franconia and the neighboring towns, with due formality, dedicated this mountain to the name of the illustrious hero of that day, LaFayette."

Lakes of the Clouds
Mount Washington, Southern Ridges

These two tiny alpine ponds in the col between *Mount Monroe* and *Mount Washington* were called Blue Ponds by the Weeks-Brackett party in 1820 (see *Presidential Range*). The lakes were later called Washingtons Punch Bowl. The present name had been given to the ponds as early as 1831, and they are indeed lakes of the clouds, the larger pond being at 5,050 feet elevation.

Lancaster   *North Country*

Lancaster is the county seat of *Coös County*. Its name was suggested by Joseph Wilder, an early settler who, along with many other settlers of the area, had come from Lancaster, Massachusetts. A party of men, mostly from Lancaster, ascended the *Presidential Range* in 1820 and gave most of the peaks there the names they bear today.

Landaff   *Cannon, Kinsman*

Landaff, east of *Lisbon*, originally was granted as Whicherville in 1764, but in 1774 it was reincorporated as Llandaff. This early spelling clearly is Welsh; the second "l" has been dropped over the years. The town received its name to honor the Bishop of Llandaff, who at that time was chaplain to King George III of England. The town was proposed as the site for Dartmouth College, but local landowners proved too stubborn in relinquishing their land claims. The name Llandaff Mountain appeared on Philip Carrigain's map of 1816.

Langdon, Mount (2,423 feet)
Mount Washington, Southern Ridges

Mount Langdon in the southern part of *Montalban Ridge* was at one time named Mount Blackwell by Lucy Stone Blackwell to honor her husband, Henry B. Blackwell. In 1876 the AMC renamed the peak to honor Dr. Samuel Langdon (1723–97), president of Harvard College and joint author with Colonel Blanchard of a map of New Hampshire.

Lary Brook, Flume; Lary Brook Mountain (2,988 feet)
Mahoosuc Range Area

Joseph Lary was an early settler in the area. The brook heads on the east side of the *Mahoosuc Range* and flows south, to the west of Lary Brook Mountain, into the *Androscoggin River*. Lary Flume is on an upper tributary of *Austin Mill Brook,* east of *Gentian Pond.*

Leadmine Brook, Reservation   *Mahoosuc Range Area*

Lead was discovered about 1820 near this brook roughly halfway between *Gorham* and *Shelburne,* and the lead mine that was opened, soon after the discovery, gave the brook its name. A piece of ore from the mine, weighing about 2,400 pounds and nearly cubical in shape, was exhibited in London in 1851 and was said to be the largest piece of pure galena ever mined. In 1935 Miss Anne Whitney of Boston and Mrs. Grace E. Kendall of New York gave 155 acres on both sides of the *Androscoggin River* to New Hampshire to be used as a public reservation, and the tract also took the mine's name.

Leavitt Brook   *North Country*

In the winter of 1818 two boys, William Horne and Edmund Leavitt, ran away from their homes in *Stark,* intending to follow the *Androscoggin River* south to *Shelburne.* Deep snow hindered their progress, and it was after dark before they could hear *Berlin Falls.* Fearing that they could not get safely around the falls, they abandoned their plans and turned homeward. At the mouth of a small brook, Leavitt collapsed from cold and exhaustion. Horne, unable to move Leavitt, left him there to go for help. He finally reached the farm of Moses Robbins, the only settler nearby, but when a rescue party reached Leavitt they were too late; he had died. The brook where he perished took his name. There is a *Horne Brook* nearby that may have been named for his companion.

Lend-a-Hand Trail   *Franconia, Twin, Willey Ranges*

Rev. Edward Everett Hale, the Boston pastor and author, also edited a journal for charitable organizations entitled *Lend-a-Hand.* This trail, named for the journal, connects the *Zealand* Falls Hut with the mountain named for its editor, *Mount Hale.*

Liberty, Mount (4,460 feet)   *Franconia, Twin, Willey Ranges*

Mounts Liberty, *Lafayette,* and *Flume* all were known to early settlers as the Haystacks, because of their shapes; see *Haystack (general).* Lucy Crawford, wife of Ethan Allen Crawford, referred in her diary to being able to see, to the south of her home at *Fabyan,* "the beautiful green hill where deer live in the summer, since named Liberty Mountain. . . ." But it is not known which mountain she was referring to because the summit that today bears that name could not be seen from Fabyan. An article in *Harper's Magazine* in 1852 mentioned the Mount Liberty in the *Franconia Range,* but it is not known exactly when or why Mount Liberty received its name.

Liberty Trail   *Chocorua, East Sandwich*

See *Jim Liberty Shelter.*

Lincoln   *Franconia, Twin, Willey Ranges*

The town of Lincoln was named in 1764 for Henry Clinton, Ninth Earl of Lincoln and a cousin of the Wentworth governors, who named so many towns in northern New Hampshire. Lincoln once was the site of intense lumbering, and loggers dubbed parts of the region with names such as Pullman, Sawdust Boulevard, and Henryville, the last name derived from the Henry Company, established in 1892 by J. E. Henry to carry out logging operations in the area; the whole region was once facetiously referred to as the Grand Duchy of Lincoln.

Lincoln, Mount (5,108 feet)   *Franconia, Twin, Willey Ranges*

A Mr. Fifield named this peak in the *Franconia Range* for President Lincoln. It had previously been called Mount Pleasant, not to be confused with the Mount Pleasant later renamed to *Mount Eisenhower.*

Lincoln Woods Trail   *Franconia, Twin, Willey Ranges*

See *Wilderness Trail.*

The Link   *Northern Peaks, Great Gulf*

J. Rayner Edmands in 1893 built this path skirting the lower northern slopes of *Mounts Madison, Adams,* and *Jefferson.* He intended it to be a connecting "link" between the Ravine House and the paths ascending *Nowell, Israel,* and *Castellated Ridges.* Memorial Bridge, which crosses Cold Brook on the Link, is a memorial to such pioneer trailmakers in the White Mountains as Cook, King, Gordon, Lowe, Watson, Peek, Hunt, Nowell, Sargent—and, of course, Edmands.

Lion Head   *Mount Washington, Southern Ridges*

Originally known as St. Anthonys Nose, this rocky prominence on the southeast shoulder of *Mount Washington* has been known since about 1875 as Lion Head, a name derived from its shape.

Lisbon   *Connecticut Region*

Lisbon is the fourth name this town south of *Littleton* has borne during its history. It was called Concord in 1763, then renamed Chiswick a year later. Three years after that it was renamed again, as Gunthwaite. It was named Lisbon in 1824, most likely at the suggestion of Gov. Levi Woodbury. His friend, Col. William Jarvis, had been consul at Lisbon, Portugal, during Jefferson's administration and was largely responsible for 3,500 merino sheep being sent to the U.S., many to New Hampshire.

Little Attitash Mountain   (2,518 feet)
Carrigain, Moat Regions

See *Attitash Mountain.*

Little Haystack Mountain   (4,513 feet)
Franconia, Twin, Willey Ranges

Early settlers referred to *Mounts Liberty, Flume, Lafayette,* and this peak as the Haystacks, because of their shapes. Mount Lafayette was known as the Great Haystack.

Littleton   *Connecticut Region*

Until 1770 this town was part of *Lisbon,* which then was called Chiswick. In that year what is now Littleton was granted by Gov. John Wentworth as Apthorp to a group of wealthy Boston merchants who purchased or were granted 40,865 acres in the White Mountains. About the time of the Revolutionary War, these lands came into the possession of Col. Moses Little, "Surveyor of the King's Woods" under Gov. Wentworth and a veteran of the French and Indian Wars and the Battle of Bunker Hill. Littleton was named for him in 1784, the same year New Hampshire became a state.

Livermore   *Carrigain, Moat Regions*

Almost all traces have vanished of the once-thriving lumber settlement that existed in this unincorporated town six miles west of *Bartlett.* The town had been incorporated in 1876, and it was named for Samuel Livermore, an early grantee of the town; he also was a delegate to the Continental Congress, first chief justice of New Hampshire, and a U.S. senator. But, despite the prominence of its eponymn and its promising beginning, the town of Livermore dwindled during this century, its population reaching zero by 1951, when its incorporation was revoked. Today, this town whose human population once depended upon the felling of trees ironically now has no human residents, and its thousands of trees are protected within the WMNF.

Locke Hill (2,105 feet)   *Mahoosuc Range Area*

Samuel Locke of Bethel, Maine, built a mill in Bethel Township in 1830 and settled near Locke Mountain. This small summit north of the *Sunday River* also bears his family name.

Lonesome Lake   *Cannon, Kinsman*

Formerly known as Tamarack Pond and as Moran Lake, the lake beneath the south shoulder of *Cannon Mountain* was given its present name by the author and editor William C. Prime (1825–1905), who had a cabin on its shores.

Long Mountain (3,640 feet)   *North Country*

The shape of this mountain in *Stratford,* especially when viewed from the west, doubtless is responsible for its name. The name Long Mountain appears on a 1788 map of Stratford.

Lost Nation   *North Country*

Next to the *Pilot Range* east of *Lancaster* is this tiny settlement that was neither lost nor a nation. Local tradition says the locality received its name from an incident in which a traveling preacher visited the area and called the people together for worship. Only one person showed up, so the preacher likened the local residents to one of the lost tribes of Israel. A less common tradition says the name was derived from an early pack peddler who found travel in the area so difficult because of the rough roads that he dubbed the area Lost Nation.

Lost River   *Moosilauke Region*

It is not surprising that this river on *Mount Moosilauke* is called Lost River because, as it tumbles down the mountain through a boulder-filled gorge, it has little choice but to "disappear" from time to time among the huge rocks and potholes. A very credible local tradition says the river was "found" by two young boys, Royal and Lyman Jackman, who had gone fishing in the valley. Suddenly, Royal later related, Lyman vanished "as though the earth had opened and swallowed him." He'd dropped a dozen feet through a hole into a waist-deep pool. Badly frightened but unhurt, he was retrieved. Many years later the aged Royal returned to North Woodstock. While there he blazed a trail through the woods with the help of some local boys, and when it was finished he took the boys to what is now the Cave of the Shadows. "This," he said, "is where my brother found the Lost River." Actually, many persons have claimed to have "found" Lost River, and exactly who first explored it can never be known. Today, the caves and potholes making Lost River unique are under the care of the SPNHF. Along Lost River is a small waterfall once called Falls of Proserpine, located in a boulder cave appropriately named the Judgment Hall of Pluto. At the other extreme of divine cosmology is another waterfall on Lost River—Paradise Falls.

Lowe and Burbanks Grant   *Northern Peaks, Great Gulf*

In 1832 Clovis Lowe of *Jefferson* and Barker Burbank of *Shelburne* purchased from the state this tract that includes *Mounts Madison* and *Sam Adams* and *Pine Mountain*. The land is now within the WMNF.

Lowell, Mount (3,743 feet)   *Carrigain, Moat Regions*

Originally called Brickhouse Mountain, this peak northeast of *Carrigain Notch* was renamed in 1869 by the New Hampshire Geological Survey for Abner Lowell of Portland, Maine, an old and enthusiastic explorer of the White Mountains.

Lower Kimball Pond   *Cater, Baldface Ranges*

See *Kimball Ponds*.

Lowes Path   *Northern Peaks, Great Gulf*

Leading from Bowman Station in *Randolph* over *Nowell Ridge* to the summit of *Mount Adams,* this path was made by Charles E. Lowe in 1875–76 from his house on Randolph Highway, and until 1880 he maintained it as a toll path. The Lowes were among the earliest settlers of Randolph—their descendants still live in the area—and Charles Lowe was a well-known guide in the region; from 1895 to his death in 1907 he was the proprietor of the Mount Crescent House at Randolph. Lowe was assisted in building the path named for him by Dr. William G. Nowell, a very active trailmaker in the White Mountains (see *Nowell Ridge*). Lowes Path is the oldest of the mountain trails originating in Randolph Valley.

Lucys Baths   *Carrigain, Moat Regions*

See *Dianas Baths*.

Lyman   *Connecticut Region*

In 1761 this town in northwestern *Grafton County* was granted to Daniel Lyman and sixty-three others, ten of whom also were named Lyman. (See also *Monroe* entry.)

L

Madison, Mount (5,363 feet)   *Northern Peaks, Great Gulf*

The most northerly peak of the *Presidential Range* was named in 1820 by the naming party from *Lancaster* that included mapmaker and New Hampshire secretary of state Philip Carrigain in honor of the nation's fourth president, James Madison (1751–1836). Madison Spring nearby was named by William G. Nowell in 1875.

Mad River   *Waterville Valley Region*

On the back of Thornton's original charter, dated 1768, is a rough map on which the name Madd River appears. The difference in spelling between Madd and Mad is inconsequential, as orthography then was a matter of individual preference; unfortunately the name's antiquity offers no clues to its origin.

The poet Henry Wadsworth Longfellow wrote a poem entitled "Mad River in the White Mountains." One of the stanzas goes like this:

> Men call me Mad, and well they may,
>   When, full of rage and trouble,
> I burst my banks of sand and clay,
> And sweep their wooden bridge away,
>   Like withered reeds or stubble.

Mad River; Mad River Falls   *Carter, Baldface Ranges*

Naming a stream "mad" is relatively common. The White Mountains have not only the well-known river in *Waterville Valley* but also this short Mad River, which heads between *East Royce Mountain* and

West Royce Mountain and flows south into *Cold River*. A Mad River also exists in Strafford County.

Magalloway River, Mountain (3,360 feet) *North Country*

"Magalloway" in the Abenaki language means "the shoveler" and refers to the caribou. The Abenakis called the caribou "shovelers" because of their habit of shoveling snow aside with their hooves to get food. So a loose translation of this river in northeastern *Coös County* would be "abode of the caribou."

Mahoosuc Notch, Range, Arm, Mountain (3,490 feet) *Mahoosuc Range Area*

Clearly of Indian origin, this name can be translated two ways, both equally plausible. In Abenaki the word means "abode of hungry animals," a phrase that could refer to numerous wild species, though it also has been suggested that the name refers to the Mohegan-Pequot refugees who fled from Connecticut to Maine following the Pequot War of 1637.

But the name Mahoosuc also approximates a word in the Natick Indian language meaning "pinnacle, mountain peak," which aptly describes the region. The AMC in 1918 approved the name for the range of mountains running northeast from the *Androscoggin River* valley at *Gorham* to *Grafton Notch* in Maine; the name previously had been applied just to Mahoosuc Notch. Mahoosuc Notch, Mountain, and Arm—a subsidiary summit of the mountain—are in the northeast part of the range.

Marshfield Station *Mount Washington, Southern Ridges*

The first white man to ascend *Mount Washington* was Darby Field, and the first and only man to put a railroad up it was Sylvester Marsh. From the joining of their two surnames came the present name for the train station servicing the Mount Washington *Cog Railway*. The station previously had been known as Kroflite Kamp. Marsh, in addition to being chief builder and promoter of the railroad, was an inventor of meat-packing machinery.

Martha, Mount (3,554 feet) *North Country*

Had it been her choice, Martha Washington probably would have preferred to have been honored with a mountain closer to the mountain named for her husband, *Mount Washington,* than this summit, the highest point on sprawling *Cherry Mountain.*

Martin Meadow Pond   *North Country*

An early hunter named Martin is the origin of the name of this pond south of the village of *Lancaster.* The names Martin Meadow Pond and Martin Meadow Hills appeared on Philip Carrigain's 1816 map of the White Mountains.

Martins Location   *Northern Peaks, Great Gulf*

Thomas Martin of Portsmouth was a conductor of artillery stores in the French and Indian Wars, and in 1773 he was among the original grantees of this tract in *Pinkham Notch.* The lands were never incorporated, and today they are notable for being the site of the *Dolly Copp Campground.*

McCrillis Path   *Chocorua, East Sandwich*

The site of the McCrillis Farm is near this path on *Mount Whiteface.*

Meserve Brook   *Mount Washington, Southern Ridges*

Prior to 1915 considerable confusion had existed as to the name of this brook running into the *Ellis River* west of *Jackson* and the name of the brook roughly paralleling it on the north. In that year, the AMC Committee on Nomenclature recommended that the brook running from Maple Mountain be called Meserve Brook and the other one *Miles Brook.* The name Meserve most likely comes from W. A. Meserve of Jackson, who in 1905 built the path to nearby *Iron Mountain.*

Metallak Island; Mount Metalak (2,699 feet)
North Country

Metallak was a chief of the Coo-ash-auke Indians who once inhabited the northern tip of New Hampshire. Legend tells that when his wife (see *Molls Rock*) died, he put her body into a canoe and went with it down rapids on the *Androscoggin River* until he came to the tiny island in *Lake Umbagog* that bears his name. There, where he buried her, he built a hut where he lived in solitude. Several years later, in 1846, some hunters found him blind and starving. They took him to *Stewartstown,* where he lingered a few years, a ward of the state. He was buried in a tiny cemetery in Stewartstown, the last of his people here. Mount Metalak in *Millsfield* recalls his presence. The island has been known as Dutton Island and Duttons Island, as well as such variants of the present name as Mettallack Island, Metallacks Island, and even Metallic Island, but in 1939 the USBGN established the present form.

Middle Moriah Mountain   (3,755 feet)
Carter, Baldface Ranges

See *Mount Moriah.*

Milan
North Country

When this town on the upper *Androscoggin River* originally was granted in 1771, it was called Paulsbourg, for Gov. John Wentworth's cousin Paul, who resided in England. Few settlers were attracted to the region, but they included Milan Harris, whose family members were among the persons who established the first woolen mills in the U.S., at Harrisville. Gov. Levi Woodbury was Milan Harris's friend, and the governor was interested in encouraging the wool industry in the state, so in 1824 he authorized applying to this town his friend's first name, his surname already having been given to another town. The main villages in the town are Milan and West Milan; nonlocal persons sometimes pronounce the name like that of the Italian city, but local pronunciation accents the first syllable, MY-lan.

Miles Brook
Mount Washington, Southern Ridges

The name of this brook running southeasterly from *Rocky Branch Ridge* into the *Ellis River* often has been mistakenly given to the brook paralleling it to the south, *Meserve Brook.* In 1915 the AMC's Committee on Nomenclature recommended the present designation. The name's origin is unknown.

Miles Brook, Notch
Speckled Mountain Region

These features northeast of *Speckled Mountain* take their name from the early Miles family here.

Millen Hill (3,360 feet) *Northern Peaks, Great Gulf*

People living in Jefferson Highlands in *Jefferson* often refer to this peak immediately east of *Mount Jefferson* as Little Bowman, probably because of its proximity to *Mount Bowman*. But in 1915 the AMC's Committee on Nomenclature recommended that it bear the name Millen Hill. The mapmaker Samuel Holland, in preparing his map of the White Mountains in 1773–74, mistakenly applied the name Millen Mountain to nearby *Mount Mitten*, seemingly because of an engraver's error. The origin of the name Millen Hill is unknown.

Millsfield *North Country*

This sparsely populated town southeast of *Dixville Notch* was named for Sir Thomas Mills of London, a prominent trader in lumber and other commodities and an advocate in Parliament of conciliation with the New England colonies. The town was granted by Gov. John Wentworth in 1774, but it was never incorporated, and by 1960 the population, never large, had declined to seven.

Mist, Mount (2,220 feet) *Moosilauke Region*

Mist sweeping upward from nearby *Lake Tarleton* in *Piermont* to this peak's summit is responsible for its name.

Mitten, Mount (3,050 feet) *North Country*

More than once in White Mountains history a seemingly trivial incident engendered an enduring and intriguing name, as the name of this mountain in the Dartmouth Range illustrates. In April 1771, according to tradition, thirty-year-old Timothy Nash was following a moose through the dense forest on this mountain when he lost his bearings. Climbing a tree to get a better view, he saw to the south the huge cleft in the mountains later to be called *Crawford Notch*. But in climbing the tree Nash lost a mitten, and for more than two centuries the name *Mount Mitten* has recalled the incident. But, while the mitten's loss may have been trivial, the discovery of Crawford Notch was important indeed (see *Crawford Notch* and *Nash and Sawyers Location*). The name Mount Mitten first appeared on the 1772 charter map of *Bretton Woods*.

Mittersill *Franconia, Twin, Willey Ranges*

In 1939 Baron Hubert von Pantz arrived in *Franconia* seeking a site on which to reconstruct the Austria he had recently fled following the Nazi "anschluss" there. Impressed with *Cannon*'s aerial tram and Taft Trail, he later said, "I wanted to create a village where the skiers could walk right out to ski without having to take a car." Soon von Pantz and his wife acquired property in *Sugar Hill*, and they set about realizing their dream; von Pantz named it for Mittersill, Austria, site of the castle of Mittersill—a well-known ski factory.

Mizpah Spring   *Mount Washington, Southern Ridges*

In Hebrew "mizpah" means "watchtower," and it is the name of several sites in ancient Palestine, especially the heap of stones erected in the mountains of Gilead by Jacob and Laban. Exactly why this spring south of *Mount Pierce*, on the Mount Clinton Trail, bears this name is unknown, but such biblical names are common throughout the U.S.

Moat Mountain (3,201 feet)   *Carrigain, Moat Regions*

Moat Mountain, an irregular ridge west of the *Saco River* nearly opposite North Conway, is actually three mountains: North Moat, 3,201 feet; Middle Moat, 2,760 feet; and South Moat, 2,772 feet; a ridge connecting North Moat with Big *Attitash* has been called West Moat. (The application of these names has been confusing). The name Moat Mountain was given by early settlers because of beaver dams along streams on the mountain's slopes. The ponds behind the dams were called moats locally, and a visit to the region was termed "going over the moats." The name appears as Mote on the 1771 charter map of *Albany*.

Mohawk River   *North Country*

Mohawk Indians are supposed to have raided in this region, and settlers named this river paralleling N.H. Route 26 east of *Colebrook* for them.

Molls Rock   *North Country*

"Molly Molasses" supposedly was a nickname the Coo-ash-auke chief Metallak (see *Metallak Island*) used for his wife. This islet in the town of *Errol* is named for her.

Molly Ocket	*Carter, Baldface Ranges*
Molledgewock Brook	*North Country*
Mollockett Brook	*North Country*

Molly Ocket was an old Sokosis Indian woman who lived and traveled throughout the White Mountains around 1800, and numerous place names recall her presence. There is a Molledgewock Brook near *Errol,* a Mollockett Brook near *Berlin,* and a Molly Lockett Cave near Fryeburg, Maine.

In *Conway* she is remembered for an incident that occurred while she was bringing some seed corn to Colonel McMillan, something she did each spring. This time, however, she laid the sack of corn by some old logs, and while she was away her corn was taken and ground into meal by mistake. This inspired a local wag to write:

> Molly Ocket lost her pocket,
> Lydia Fisher found it,
> Lydia carried it to the mill,
> And Uncle Noah ground it.

Even without the corn mishap, however, Molly Ocket would be remembered in Conway. She once saved the life of a Boston fur trader by warning him of a death plot by an Indian named Tomhegan. To save the trader, Molly Ocket had to make a long journey through the wilderness, but the trader acknowledged and later rewarded her courage.

About 1774 she moved to the Bethel, Maine, area, where her name was spelled Mollyockett, but she continued to practice Indian medicine and to perform charitable acts; citizens of Bethel still observe an annual Mollyockett Day in her memory. She died in 1816 and was buried in Andover, Maine, under her Christian name of Mary Agatha.

Monroe   *Connecticut Region*

Hurds Location, for John Hurd, was the original name of this town south and west of *Littleton;* later it was known as West Lyman, the town then being part of the town of *Lyman.* Lyman was divided in 1854, and, when it became clear that a new name would be needed for the western portion, a dispute arose among area residents. John Hurd's descendants wanted the town to be named again for him, and they had a strong argument. Hurd had been secretary to Gov. John Wentworth and very active in the affairs of the territory's northern part. Members of his family were grantees of several nearby towns, including Lyman, *Bath, Haverhill, Lisbon,* and *Whitefield.* But another faction wanted the town named for James Monroe, fifth president, who had toured New Hampshire during his term, and the Monroe advocates eventually prevailed.

Monroe, Mount (5,385 feet)
Mount Washington, Southern Ridges

In 1820, when mapmaker and New Hampshire secretary of state Philip Carrigain and the Weeks-Brackett party from *Lancaster* named *Presidential Range* peaks, James Monroe (1758–1831), the nation's fifth president, was in office, and they named this summit southwest of *Mount Washington* for him. A crag near the summit is called Little Monroe.

Montalban Ridge
Mount Washington, Southern Ridges

Moses F. Sweetser, in his 1876 White Mountains guide, labeled as Montalban this long ridge approaching *Mount Washington* from the south. The name is simply a Latinization of "white mountain," and indeed, the name has appeared as Mount Alban; in 1978 the USBGN accepted the one-word form. "White Mountain" is perhaps the world's most common mountain name (see *White Mountains*); Montalban is the New England equivalent of Mauna Kea in Hawaii, Mont Blanc in the Alps, Craig Eyri and Snowdon in Wales, Ben Nevis in Scotland, and Dhaulagiri in the Himalayas.

Monticello Lawn
Northern Peaks, Great Gulf

On the south shoulder of *Mount Jefferson* is a smooth, grassy plateau named in 1876 by Moses F. Sweetser in allusion to Thomas Jefferson's estate in Virginia.

Moose Brook State Park
North Country

The presence of moose here—or an incident involving one—doubtless accounts for this name. The name Moose River appeared on Samuel Holland's 1784 map. The region was once known locally as Heaths District.

Moosilauke, Mount (4,810 feet)
Moosilauke Region

As happened so often with place names derived from Indian words, Moosilauke has been spelled literally dozens of ways in its history, with Mooshillock, Mooselock, Mooshelock, and Mooseelauke being only a few of the variants; in 1911 the USBGN established Moosilauke as the accepted form. The most common derivation is from two Abenaki words: "moosi" meaning "bald" and "-auke" meaning "place." But other possible translations include "at the place of the ferns," "good moose place along the brook," and "at the smooth place on the summit." Also unsettled is whether the name should be pronounced to rhyme with "rock" or "rocky."

Tradition has it that the Abenaki chief Waternomee ascended the peak in 1685. And Robert Pomeroy, one of Rogers's Rangers, is reported to have died on the mountain in 1759. Amos F. Clough, a photographer, and Prof. J. H. Huntington, of the New Hampshire Geological Survey, spent the winter of 1869–70 on the summit of Mount Moosilauke and thus became pioneers in the field of mountain meteorology.

Moosilauke Brook   *Moosilauke Region*

This short brook formed by the confluence of *Lost River,* Walker Brook, and *Jackman Brook,* entering the *Pemigewasset River* from the west at North Woodstock, was named for *Mount Moosilauke* to the west.

Moriah Brook, Gorge; Mount (4,047 feet)
Carter, Baldface Ranges

Moriah Mountain, Middle (3,755 feet)

Moriah Mountain, Shelburne (3,735 feet)

In the Bible, Moriah is identified both as the hill in ancient Palestine on which Abraham prepared to sacrifice Isaac and as the hill in the eastern part of Jerusalem on which Solomon built the Temple. Moriah in Hebrew means "provided by Jehovah," and it is thought these mountains south of *Gorham* received their names from an early settler familiar with these meanings. The name first appeared on Philip Carrigain's map of 1816. Middle Moriah Mountain is on the ridge between Mount Moriah and Shelburne Moriah Mountain, named for being south of the village of *Shelburne.* Moriah Brook, named for the mountains, heads south of them and runs southeast into *Wild River,* flowing through Moriah Gorge and creating a scenic cascade.

Morrison Brook
Carter, Baldface Ranges

This short tributary of *Evans Brook* bears the name of an early family in the area.

Moses Rock
Mahoosuc Range Area

In the middle of *Shelburne* is a huge smooth ledge on the side of what is now Mount Winthrop. During an early survey, according to tradition, the best lot in town was offered to the man who could first climb this rock. A man named Moses Ingalls (see *Mount Ingalls*) thereupon took off his shoes and ran barefoot up the rock. He received, in addition to the lot, the distinction of having the rock named for him.

Mother Walker Falls
Mahoosuc Range Area

Mother Walker is said to have been a homesteader in the Grafton, Maine, area, arriving late in the nineteenth century, when the area was growing rapidly because of the softwood pulp industry. She owned the land surrounding these falls on the Bear River southeast of *Grafton Notch*.

Mountain Pond
Carter, Baldface Ranges

The name of this pond east of the *Doubleheads* simply describes its location in a small valley surrounded by mountains. The WMNF has created the Mountain Pond Research Natural Area here.

Muise Mountain (3,610 feet)
North Country

In 1971 the Groveton Fish and Game Club mounted an effort to have an unnamed peak in the wilderness south of *Dixville Notch* named for Arthur Muise, a popular local conservation officer. The effort was successful, and officer Muise became probably the only living person in New Hampshire able to enjoy the honor of having a mountain named for him. He retired from conservation work soon after the naming.

Muscanigra Falls
Northern Peaks, Great Gulf

These obscure falls on upper *Bumpus Brook* commemorate one of the most ubiquitous and certainly the most infamous creatures of the White Mountains—the black fly (Latin, "musca," meaning "fly," "nigra," meaning "black").

Nancy Brook, Cascades, Pond; Mount (3,906 feet)
Carrigain, Moat Regions

Nancy Barton was a young servant at the estate of Col. Joseph Whipple in Dartmouth, now *Jefferson*. It would not have been an easy life for the young maid, for Colonel Whipple was regarded as a hard master, but while she was at his estate she fell in love with a man tradition says was named Jim Swindell.

Colonel Whipple is said to have discovered the romance—and disapproved—so, on a cold December day in 1778, Colonel Whipple arranged for Nancy's lover to be transferred to Portsmouth while Nancy was in nearby *Lancaster*. When Nancy returned and found her lover gone, she fled the estate and pursued him. She got as far as the brook in *Crawford Notch* that bears her name. There she was later found, frozen in a sitting position, her head resting on her hand and walking cane, her clothing frozen to her body from having walked across the stream.

It is uncertain whether Swindell had left her faithlessly or not, but legend says he was so unsettled by her death that he died shortly after in an insane asylum.

This tale, which is believable at least regarding Colonel Whipple, was first printed in Dwight's *Travels* of 1797. A Harvard Latinist once proposed changing the name of Mount Nancy to Mount Amoris-gelu, "the frost of love," but fortunately his idea came to naught.

Nancy Pond and Nancy Brook have been designated Research Natural Areas by the WMNF.

Nash and Sawyers Location *Franconia, Twin, Willey Ranges*

Benjamin Sawyer and Capt. Timothy Nash were two pioneer settlers who achieved a place in history because of a moose hunt. In

April 1771, Nash was pursuing a moose on what today is called *Mount Mitten* when he lost his way. He climbed a tree to get his bearings (losing a mitten in the process and thus naming the mountain), when he spied what appeared to be a notch in the mountains to the south. Nash at the time was a resident of nearby Lunenburg, Vermont, and he knew well what the discovery of a route through the White Mountains would mean to the development of the North Country. He lost no time in exploring the notch and in proving that it did indeed go through the mountains. He carried the news to Gov. John Wentworth, who was also interested and excited. But Governor Wentworth was cautious, too; he had heard other promising but ultimately disappointing tales of the long-sought-after notch, so he agreed to support and reward Nash only if Nash could bring a horse through the notch. (Some versions of the story say the horse was to be laden with rum.)

Nash readily accepted the challenge, and he returned to the North Country where he enlisted the aid of Benjamin Sawyer. It was no easy task they undertook. At one point they had to lower the horse over a cliff with ropes, and it is not recorded whether the rum casks were empty or full when they arrived in Portsmouth.

But arrive they did! And Governor Wentworth kept his word by giving them in 1773 this strip of land running north from *Crawford Notch* to slightly beyond *Fabyan*. They also received grants in *Bath*, *Conway, Lancaster,* and *Northumberland*; they sold their grant near Crawford Notch the same year they received it. Eleazer Rosebrook of Guildhall, Vermont, settled on the site of their grant—he brought the first commercial load through the notch, a barrel of rum brought from Portland to Lancaster to trade for a barrel of tobacco—and in 1803 the Tenth New Hampshire Turnpike was built through Crawford Notch—thirty-two years after Nash discovered it.

Nash Stream   *North Country*

Heading at Nash Bog Pond east of *Sugarloaf* and flowing south into the *Upper Ammonoosuc River,* this major drainage may take its name from Capt. Timothy Nash, an early settler (see *Nash and Sawyers Location*), though this origin is not certain. Long owned by timber companies, much land along the drainage has passed into public ownership to protect what Moses F. Sweetser saw when he wrote in 1887: "The narrow valley of Nash's Stream is cloven through this rugged and desolate region. . . . The character of the view in this direction is wild and primeval."

Nathans Pond *North Country*

A supposedly true tale of true grit is behind the name of this pond in *Stewartstown*. Nathan Caswell was an old hunter who camped on the shores of the pond, and one winter day he cut his foot with an axe. Immobilized by the wound and unable to summon help or expect rescue, he could only watch his provisions dwindle, and he soon faced starvation. One day he heard a dog bark, and, taking a gun and crawling toward the sound, he saw a bear in a tree. He shot the bear—no small feat in his condition—and the meat kept him alive until he could try to make his way toward the settlements. He rolled himself in the bear's skin for warmth, but the skin froze, and he had trouble getting free. He traveled the last eight miles to help crawling on his hands and knees.

Nelson Crag *Mount Washington, Southern Ridges*

In 1870–71 an expedition that included S. A. Nelson of Georgetown, Massachusetts, spent the winter on *Mount Washington*. This was the first party to spend a winter on the mountain, and the overlook on *Huntington Ravine* (see entry) from the northeastern shoulder of Mount Washington was named for Nelson.

New River *Mount Washington, Southern Ridges*

Avalanches and landslides many times have twisted and interrupted this stream draining into the *Ellis River* from the *Gulf of Slides*. The river may have broken free from a natural earth dam in 1775, for in that year Dr. Jeremy Belknap wrote in his journal that the river "broke forth . . . ; it forms a cascade upwards of 100 feet, visible at its descent into Ellis River." This "newness" of the river would easily explain its name. Avalanches altered the course of the river in 1776 and again in 1826, and possibly many more times.

Noon Peak (approx. 2,950 feet) *Waterville Valley Region*

Early residents near this peak once used it as a crude sundial, for at midday the sun stood right over it—hence the name.

North Kinsman (4,293 feet) *Cannon, Kinsman*

See *Mount Kinsman*.

Northumberland *North Country*

In 1761 Gov. Benning Wentworth gave this town on the *Upper Ammonoosuc River* the name Stonington, probably after Stonington, Connecticut. Only ten years later, his nephew Gov. John Wentworth renamed it Northumberland for Hugh Smithson, Earl Percy and First Duke of Northumberland. The nearby settlement of *Percy* is named for the same man. Smithson was pro-colonial in the dispute between King George III and the colonies, and his son James helped found the new nation's greatest academy of sciences, the Smithsonian Institution, which was named for him.

Notchland *Franconia, Twin, Willey Ranges*

In *Harts Location,* slightly south of *Crawford Notch* and on the west side of U.S. Route 3 is a stone house built around 1840 by the Boston dentist Dr. Samuel Bemis (see *Mount Bemis*), who spent his summers in Harts Location from 1827 to 1840. After building the stone house known as Notchland, Dr. Bemis lived there year-round. He came to be known as the "Lord of the Valley," and his life intertwined with that of the colorful Crawford family. He owned a considerable amount of land in the valley, and he was responsible for the naming of many features in the area, including *Mount Crawford, Mount Resolution,* and *Giant Stairs.*

Nowell Ridge *Northern Peaks, Great Gulf*

Dr. William G. Nowell was a very active trailbuilder in the White Mountains. He was First Councilor of Improvements for the AMC from 1876 to 1878, and he laid out an extensive scheme of pathwork. A summer resident of *Randolph,* he helped Charles E. Lowe cut his path up *Mount Adams* in 1875 (see *Lowes Path*), and the next year Dr. Nowell built the first camp on the Northern Peaks. This northwest ridge of Mount Adams was named for him.

No. 13 Falls *Franconia, Twin, Willey Ranges*

Often abbreviated simply 13 Falls, this name aptly describes the waterfalls on *Franconia Brook* near its head southeast of *Mount Garfield.*

Oakes Gulf   *Southern Peaks*

William Oakes (1799–1848) first visited the White Mountains while he was a twenty-six-year-old Harvard law student, a trip he made with Charles Pickering, then a young Harvard medical student. Oakes became so engrossed in botany that he dropped law to devote his time to working on the flora of New England, and his beautifully displayed specimens were widely distributed. In 1848 he published *Scenery of the White Mountains,* with illustrations by Godfrey N. Frankenstein and Isaac Sprague, and he was planning a guidebook when he met an untimely death by falling from a ferryboat in Boston Harbor, just five days after *Scenery of the White Mountains* was published. This gulf southeast of *Mount Monroe* was named for him by Prof. Edward Tuckerman, a fellow botanist.

Odell   *North Country*

The unincorporated town of Odell, comprising nearly 24,000 acres east of *Stratford,* was granted in 1834 to Richard Odell of *Conway* for $1,863. In 1940 the town had eighty-two residents, but by 1960 it had none.

Ogontz Lake   *Ogontz Lake*

This pond on *Mill Brook* in the town of *Lyman* originally was called Youngs Pond, for John Young, who came to Lyman from *Lisbon* around 1812 and settled near the pond later to bear his name. Young died in 1861 at the age of seventy. Later the pond was called Ogontz Lake, supposedly taking the name of an Indian chief.

The Old Man of the Mountain

Franconia, Twin, Willey Ranges

The origin of the name of this rock prominence on *Cannon Mountain*, also called Profile Mountain, is self-evident. The Old Man is both the official and unofficial symbol of New Hampshire, and each year thousands of persons travel through *Franconia Notch* to view the face made famous by Nathaniel Hawthorne's story, "The Great Stone Face." Daniel Webster, a native son of New Hampshire, once said: "Men hang out signs indicative of their respective trades. Shoemakers hang out a gigantic shoe; jewelers a monster watch; and the dentist hangs a gold tooth. But in the mountains of New Hampshire, God Almighty has hung out a sign to show that there He makes men."

Old Mast Road

Chocorua, East Sandwich

The Old Mast Road runs between *Mount Wonalancet* and Mounts Mexico and *Paugus*. It is said to have been built for hauling out the tallest white pine logs to serve as masts for ships of the king's navy in colonial days.

Old Shag Camp

Chocorua, East Sandwich

"Old Shag" was an early name for *Mount Paugus,* hence the name for this camp just below the summit ledges on Paugus's eastern side.

Old Speck (4,180 feet)

Mahoosuc Range Area

According to the *Dictionary of Maine Place-names,* Old Speck, third highest summit in Maine, takes its name from diverse species of trees here, giving the mountain a "speckled" appearance, especially in the fall. Speck Pond is southwest of the summit.

Oliverian Brook

Chocorua, East Sandwich

The name Oliverian Brook appeared on maps as early as 1776. It is said to be derived from a man named Oliver falling into the stream. Another Oliverian Brook is west of Glencliff and north of Webster Slide Mountain; Oliverian Notch is nearby.

Olympic Pool

Franconia, Twin, Willey Ranges

The Bolnicks, in their *Waterfalls of the White Mountains,* called this pool at *No. 13 Falls* "one of the most impressive in the whole region," and they dubbed it Olympic Pool. It remains to be seen whether this name will stick, but it is through a process such as this that many features in the White Mountains have been named.

Ore Hill (2,025 feet)   *Cannon, Kinsman*

In 1805 an iron-ore vein said to be the nation's richest was discovered at this hill 0.5 miles south of the village of *Sugar Hill*. Mining operations flourished until 1850, when competition from the West made the mine unprofitable.

Oscar, Mount (2,748 feet)   *Franconia, Twin, Willey Ranges*

Southwest of *Fabyan* is this low mountain, named for Oscar G. Barron, for many years manager of the Fabyan House. The Barrons were innkeepers throughout the White Mountains; the hotels they owned or managed included not just the Fabyan House but also the Mount Pleasant House, the Crawford House, the Twin Mountain House, and the Summit House.

Osceola, Mount (4,340 feet)   *Waterville Valley Region*

This peak south of *Kancamangus Pass* has an Indian name whose meaning is known—but not how it got here. Osceola has nothing to do with any New Hampshire Indians, referring instead to the Seminole chief in the Florida Everglades who led his people in stubborn resistance against the whites and was finally captured in Georgia in 1837. The name itself was derived from the Seminole "asi-yaholo," meaning literally "black drink" but also referring to a ceremonial potion. Nathaniel L. Goodrich, in his history of *Waterville Valley,* suggests that both *Mount Tecumseh* and Mount Osceola were named by E. J. Connable of Jackson, Michigan, who came to Waterville in 1859. The main mountain of Osceola has two subordinate summits: East Peak, 4,156 feet, and West Peak, 4,114 feet.

Osgood Trail, Ridge   *Northern Peaks, Great Gulf*

Benjamin F. Osgood was a famous guide at the *Glen House* in the late 1800s, and in 1878 he with others opened the path leading from the Glen House to *Mount Madison*. This path, and the ridge it follows, were named for him. Though a portion of the path's lower end has been relocated, the trail's remaining sections are the oldest route still in use to the Mount Madison summit. The Osgood Cutoff is a shortcut between the *Great Gulf* and Madison Gulf trails and the Osgood Trail.

Owlhead Mountain (approx. 2,925 feet)   *North Country*

This peak between Potters Pond and the *Percy Peaks* in *Stratford* has a descriptive metaphor for a name.

Owls Head (4,025 feet)   *Franconia, Twin, Willey Ranges*

There are at least four Owls Heads in the White Mountains: one forming the north peak of *Cherry Mountain*; one in the *Moosilauke* region; one in the North Country; and this one, the highest, south of *Mount Garfield*. All received their names because of their shapes, this near the peak's south end.

O

113

Owls Head (1,967 feet)   *Moosilauke Region*

Like the three other similarly named summits in the White Mountains, this ridge east of East *Haverhill* north of Glencliff was named for its resemblance to an owl's head.

Owls Head (3,263 feet)   *North Country*

This knob on the north slope of *Cherry Mountain* is one of four summits in the White Mountains named for their resemblance to an owl's head.

Oxford County

When David Leonard arrived here as an early settler, he gave to the settlement, the township, and eventually the county the name of the place from whence he had come—Oxford, Massachusetts. The county includes the portion of the White Mountains in Maine.

Page Hill, Pond
Mahoosuc Range Area

A hunter named Yager Page made a large clearing near this mountain in the town of *Success* in the early 1800s, and about 1823 there was a log cabin at the site, the only house in the town. Five families dwelt there. Page Hill is a name that occurs at seven other New Hampshire locations, including *Lancaster*.

Paradise Falls
Moosilauke Region

See *Lost River.*

Parapet Trail
Northern Peaks, Great Gulf

This trail around the south side of the *Mount Madison* summit takes its name from a ledge, called the Parapet, overlooking Madison Gulf.

Partridge Lake
Connecticut Region

Two explanations exist for the name of Partridge Lake, located west of *Littleton* and the only natural water body in the town to be called a lake. The 1905 *History of Littleton* says it was named for Nathaniel Partridge, born 1767, who settled in *Lyman* at the lake's outlet. But the 1898 *Littleton and the White Mountains,* compiled by Paul Clay, says it was named for William Partridge, an "old-time resident who once owned a large part of the land" enclosing the pond. Most likely, Nathaniel was the original eponymn. The area once abounded in moose, and wolves roamed here; in 1800 Nathaniel Partridge, returning from a visit to a friend, was pursued by a large pack of wolves and spent the night taking refuge in a tree.

Passaconaway, Mount (4,060 feet)

In the language of the Penacook Indians, the name Passaconaway was really "papisse-conwa," and it meant "papoose bear" or "bear cub." But there was nothing cublike about the Passaconaway who is remembered by history. Passaconaway became chief of the Penacooks in 1620, and under his leadership the Penacooks ruled a powerful federation of tribes living mostly in what is now New Hampshire. War, famine, and pestilence had decimated the Indians a few years prior to Passaconaway's succession, but the tribes still numbered thirteen, according to some estimates, and their leader became an almost legendary figure. Legend says, for example, that at the moment of his death he "translated" to heaven from the summit of *Mount Washington* in a sled drawn by wolves. Legend also says that, just before his death, Passaconaway warned his fellow Indians not to quarrel with their English neighbors or they would be destroyed in the ensuing conflict. His son, Wonalancet (see *Wonalancet*), did not heed his words and in 1689 led an attack on Dover; pursued into Maine, he sued for peace in 1691, and soon thereafter most of the Penacooks left the White Mountains for Quebec. Passaconaway's grandson, Kancamagus (see *Kancamagus*), attempted peaceful relations with the English, but he, too, failed and retreated to Canada. Passaconaway's admonition had proved true. Passaconaway remained chief of the Penacooks until 1669, and he lived until 1682.

The mountain north of *Whiteface* bearing his name was once called North Whiteface. The name Passaconaway was once applied to the mountain now known as *Tripyramid*.

P

115

Pasture Path

Today a hiker might wonder at the irony of the name Pasture Path on a trail leading through dense forest, but, when this trail connecting Randolph Hill Road with the Ledge Trail was built, originally by Elliot Torrey, a summer resident of *Randolph*, the path wound among the farms of Randolph Hill.

Paugus Brook, Pass; Mount (3,200 feet)

On May 8, 1725, Capt. John Lovewell led a party of thirty-four men from Dunstable, Massachusetts, in an attack on an Indian village at the head of a pond near what is now Fryeburg. The Indians were

Sokosis, natives of the region, and they were led by their under-chief, Paugus. The battle has been called Lovewell's Massacre and justly so, for in it about sixty Indians and eighteen whites were killed, including both Lovewell and Paugus.

Mount Paugus, an irregular mass west of *Mount Chocorua,* was once called Old Shag because of the many ledges on it. The History of Carroll County says other names for Mount Paugus have included Hunchback, Deer, Frog, Middle, Berry, and Bald. The present name was suggested by Lucy Larcom, a young poet who was a summer visitor in the White Mountains and a protégé of John Greenleaf Whittier.

Peabody Brook   *Mahoosuc Range Area*

Like *Peabody Mountain* to the south, this south-flowing tributary of the *Androscoggin* recalls Oliver and John Peabody, chief proprietors of what is now *Gilead* Township, formerly the Peabody Grant.

Peabody Mountain (2,462 feet)   *Speckled Mountain Region*

The name of this mountain south of *Gilead,* Maine, recalls Oliver and John Peabody, who obtained the Peabody Grant in what is now the township of Gilead.

Peabody River   *Carter, Baldface Ranges*

Early guidebooks tell of a Mr. Peabody of Andover, Maine. He was passing the night in an Indian cabin at the height of land between the *Saco* and *Androscoggin* watersheds when suddenly he and the Indians were aroused from sleep by a roaring nearby. They escaped from the cabin just in time to watch it be swept away by a torrent that had sprung from the hillside, a natural dam having given way. Perhaps, but the river clearly antedates this incident, and the name Peabody River is old, appearing on Samuel Holland's 1784 map.

Pearl Lake   *Cannon, Kinsman*

Originally this pond near *Lisbon* was called Bear Pond, because of the numerous bears here. Then it was called Mink Pond, for the numerous mink. And finally it was called Pearl Pond—for the "pearls." In the summer of 1854 some fishermen discovered in clamshells "some substances which imagination easily manufactured into pearls." Rumor spread that a man named True Page found a pearl worth $30, and a "pearl rush" was on. Piles of discarded clamshells began to grow on the shore, and for days between fifty and seventy-five people could be seen knee-deep in the pond's water, looking for the pearl-bearing clams. They found few, if any.

Peboamauk Fall

In Abenaki "peboamauk" translates to mean "wintry place," or "winter's home," and the name is appropriate for these falls. They are on the southeast side of the *Crescent Range*, in *Ice Gulch*, a deep cut in the mountain that receives little sunlight and thereby remains cool enough to allow ice to exist even in summer.

P

117

Pemigewasset, Mount (2,554 feet) *Cannon, Kinsman*

This mountain on the east side of *Franconia Notch* has a double association with Indians. The mountain takes its name from the *Pemigewasset River* to the south, whose name is derived from an Abenaki word meaning "swift current" or "rapids." But the mountain also has on its northwest shoulder the famous Indian Head, a natural rock formation that resembles the profile of an Indian. The name Pemigewasset Mountain first appeared on a map prepared for Eastman's *White Mountain Guide* of 1863.

Pemigewasset River *Franconia, Twin, Willey Ranges*

Affectionately called "the Pemi" by hikers, the Pemigewasset River takes its name from the Abenaki Indian word "pamijowasik," meaning "swift, extended current" or "rapids." The East Branch of the Pemigewasset was called Merrimack by mapmaker Philip Carrigain in 1816. A map printed in 1767 called the river the Pemijawsitts River. These early transliterations of the Indian name use a "j," indicating that pronouncing the modern name with a soft "g" is closer to the Indian pronunciation.

Pemigewasset Wilderness Area
Fanconia, Twin, Willey Ranges

Designated in 1984, this 45,000-acre USFS wilderness area takes its name from the river whose headwaters it includes.

Pequawket (village), Pond

Chocorua, East Sandwich

Pequawket was a village of Sokosis Indians, a tribe that lived in the region that included this pond two miles west of *Conway,* drained by Pequawket Brook. The Indian word "pe-que-auk-et" has been variously translated to mean "clear valley lands bordering a crooked stream" and "broken land." Pequawket was an early name for Conway; today a tiny community northeast of *Chocorua Lake* has that name. See *Kearsarge North.*

The Perch

Northern Peaks, Great Gulf

At an elevation of 4,300 feet and "perched" on the northeast slope of *Mount Adams,* this camp was the highest of three built by the noted White Mountains trailmaker J. Rayner Edmands (see *Edmands, Col, Path*). It was named by him in 1892.

Percy (village), Pond, Peaks (3,418 feet)

North Country

The Percy Peaks, twin sugarloaf summits northeast of *Groveton,* took their names from the nearby village of Percy, once much larger than the present tiny settlement. The village was named for Hugh Smithson, Earl Percy and First Duke of Northumberland (1715–86); the nearby town of *Northumberland* was named for the same man. The English nobleman was a friend of the American colonies and argued against the policies of King George III. The Percy Peaks and Percy Pond appeared on Philip Carrigain's map of 1816.

Phillips Brook

North Country

Old residents of the area say this brook, a tributary of the *Upper Ammonoosuc River,* derives its name from King Philip, an Indian chief who sold most of northern New Hampshire to three white men. The *History of Stark,* however, gives as the origin a Mr. Phillips who, along with a man named Francis Lang, moved to the area from Saco, Maine, and built the first mill on the brook in the 1820s. Neither explanation has received corroboration from other records or informants, although Phillips Brook appeared on Philip Carrigain's 1816 map, suggesting the name predated the arrival of Mr. Phillips.

Pickering, Mount (1,945 feet)

Mount Washington, Southern Ridges

This mountain was named Pickering on Charles H. Hitchcock's 1876 map, and it commemorates a family long devoted to the

White Mountains. Charles Pickering (1805–78) was, among other things, a naturalist, and in 1838–42 he was chief zoologist on the U.S. expedition to the Antarctic and the northwest coast of America. He was twenty when he first climbed *Mount Washington* in 1825 with William Oakes, and he continued to explore the White Mountains with enthusiasm for many years, often with his close friend, Prof. William Dandridge Peck.

His love of the mountains continued in his nephews, Edward Charles Pickering (1846–1919) and Edward's brother, William Henry Pickering (1858–1938), both noted astronomers. Several features in the White Mountains were named by William Pickering, and to E. Charles Pickering, as he was known, belongs an additional achievement. He had been exploring the mountains for several years, and he enjoyed the company of persons who shared his interests. So, on January 1, 1876, E. Charles Pickering, then Thayer Professor of Physics at the Massachusetts Institute of Technology (MIT), formally invited fifty persons to a meeting of "those interested in mountain exploration." Prof. Charles E. Fay was chairman of this preliminary meeting, which was held at MIT on January 8. The first regular meeting was held on February 9, when a permanent organization was formed, There were thirty-nine charter members, and E. Charles Pickering was chosen the group's first president. The club was the Appalachian Mountain Club (AMC).

P

119

Today the AMC has thousands of members, and no other organization has had such an intimate and constructive association with the White Mountains. Its members have built trails, huts, and shelters; they have studied the mountains and written guides to their exploration and enjoyment; and most important they have constantly endeavored to keep the White Mountains the kind of wild natural area that the Pickerings found exciting over a hundred years ago.

Pickett Henry Mountain (approx. 2,150 feet)
Speckled Mountain Region

Minor summit southeast of *Gilead*, Maine, named for Pickett Henry, early settler.

Pierce, Mount (4,310 feet)
Mount Washington, Southern Ridges

Only time will tell which of two "official" names of this peak ultimately will survive. The peak east of *Crawford Notch* originally was called Mount Clinton after Gov. DeWitt Clinton of New York (1769–

1828), but in 1913 the name was changed by the New Hampshire legislature to Mount Pierce; the USBGN recognized the change. The lawmakers wanted to honor Franklin Pierce, fourteenth president and the "only citizen or resident of New Hampshire who has been the incumbent of that exalted office." Mapmakers and hikers, however, ignored the change, and in 1915 the AMC Committee on Nomenclature recommended using the old name on AMC maps. The result has been confusion, and the problem is compounded on maps showing the Mount Clinton Trail leading to Mount Pierce! To Abel Crawford, the matter was simple: he called the mountain Bald Hill.

Piermont   *Connecticut Region*

The origin of the name of this town on the *Connecticut River* is obscure. It has been suggested the name is a corruption of "piedmont," a geographical term referring to a plain lying near a mountain range, and Piermont, in some respects, does indeed resemble a piedmont. But no firm evidence exists supporting this as the name's origin, and without such evidence the true origin of the name must be said to be unknown.

Pike   *Connecticut Region*

This tiny village in southern *Haverhill* owes its name to Alonzo Pike, who had the good fortune of being shown an immense rock bed of "Bethlehem gneiss" by New Hampshire state geologist, Prof. Charles H. Hitchcock. The stone made excellent sharpening stones, and throughout the world tool grinders and sharpeners produced in northern New Hampshire were know as "Pikestones." The Alonzo Pike Company was formed in 1860, and at one time no fewer than sixteen members of the Pike family lived in the village, most of them working for the company. A declining market and exhaustion of the mineral deposit meant the eventual end of the business, though the village, where many houses were built by the company, survives.

Pike Pond   *North Country*

People, not pickerel, were responsible for the name of this pond north of the village of *Percy* on the *Upper Ammonoosuc River*. The pond was named for its first owners, the Pike family.

Pilot Range; Mount (3,710 feet)

Many local people—and many maps and guides—call this prominent peak in the Pilot Range Hutchins Mountain, named for Alpheus Hutchins, an early settler who served under Capt. John Weeks of *Lancaster* in the Battle of Chippewa in the War of 1812. But the name accepted by the USBGN and the AMC is Pilot Mountain, which gave its name to the range at whose northern end the summit is located. Far-ranging hunters and scouts journeying along the upper *Connecticut River* used these mountains as landmarks, and they called them the Land Pilot Hills. This name was in use as early as 1814, though the town plan of Percy, made about 1803, refers to Land of Pilot Mountain and doubtless means Mount Pilot, the second highest summit in the range; *Mount Cabot*, 4,180 feet, is the highest. Local legend says the name Mount Pilot is derived from the name of the dog of Jonathan Willard, an eccentric recluse who lived in the wilderness near the notch that now bears his name (see *Willard Basin, Notch*), but the prior history of the name Pilot Mountain belies this legend. The Pilot Range was called Little Moosehillock by Timothy Dwight, who passed through the region in 1797 and again in 1803.

Pine Mountain (2,404 feet)

Once called Camels Hump and Camels Rump, this mountain in Randolph takes its present name from the fine stands of pines that stood on the mountain before fires destroyed most of them. Though GNIS lists fifteen Pine Hills in New Hampshire, the state has only two Pine Mountains, and this is one of them.

Pinkhams Grant, Pinkham Notch
Mount Washington, Southern Ridges

The resourcefulness and hardiness of the early White Mountains settlers are nowhere better illustrated than in the lives of Capt. Joseph Pinkham and his son Daniel. The captain, his wife, and four children left Madbury to homestead in what is now *Jackson*, which at that time was called, not surprisingly, New Madbury. They arrived April 6, 1789, and here is how Joseph later recalled their arrival at the homestead to his son Daniel, who in 1789 would have been ten years old:

> The snow was five feet deep on the level. There was no road to Barlett, and we traveled on the snow. Our provisions, furniture, and clothing were on a handsled, to which the boys had

harnessed the hog, their only animal, and he did efficient service. On arriving at our home we found the log house erected the previous autumn half-buried in snow, and had to shovel a way through to find the door. The house had no chimney, no stove, no floor, no window, except the open door, or the smoke-hole in the roof. We built a fireplace at one end of green logs and replaced them as they burned out, until the snow left us so that we could get rocks to supply their place. We had but two chairs and one bedstead. Thus we lived until summer, when we moved the balance of our furniture from Conway. There was much poverty here at this early period, and the means of living scarce. A few families had cows, and could afford the luxury of milk porridge, but many were obliged to make their porridge of meal and water only. The rivers afforded trout, and these constituted a large portion of our food. They were dried in the sun and roasted by the fire, and eaten usually without salt, as that was a scarce article in the new settlement."

Daniel grew up on the family homestead in Jackson, and later he built a blacksmith shop there. Although Daniel never formally learned any trade, he became a blacksmith, a mason, a carpenter, a wheelwright, and even a dentist. But his subsequent fame rests on his attempts to be a roadbuilder. Under an agreement with the State of New Hampshire, Daniel was to build a road through the notch that would connect Jackson with *Gorham*. His father, Joseph, had begun such a road in 1789. Daniel was given three years to complete the task, and if he succeeded he was to receive a tract of land one-half mile wide on each side of the road from Jackson to Gorham, as well as all the state lands in the town of Jackson. But the road would be twelve miles long, through a nightmare of boulders, streams, dense timber, and steep, rugged terrain.

Two years later Daniel Pinkham had his road nearly completed, but heavy rains in August 1826 caused huge landslides that destroyed much of his progress. He abandoned the project. Later, he did construct a toll road through the notch, but deep snows discouraged travel, and this project, too, was not a financial success for him.

In 1829, at the age of fifty, Daniel Pinkham moved his family from Jackson to Pinkham's Grant and homesteaded anew. He lived there for six years. Finally, in 1834, after ten years of toil, disappointment, and poverty, his grant was confirmed, and in the speculations of 1835–36 he sold enough land to enable him to buy a farm in *Lancaster*. There he died in June 1855.

Pinkham Notch was known by that name as early as 1851. Before that it was known as Pinkham Woods, and it also has been called *The Glen*. At the time of Dr. Jeremy Belknap's expedition in 1784, it was simply the Eastern Pass, and the only route through it was a trail, known as the Shelburne Road, blazed in 1774 by Capt. John Evans, who was Belknap's guide (see *Evans Brook, Notch*).

Piper Hill, Trail   *Chocorua, East Sandwich*

Joshua Piper was one of the "Piper Boys" who ran a stagecoach near *Mount Chocorua*, and he cut the first trail—the Piper Trail—up the mountain. He later used the trail in guiding hiking parties up the mountain and also on bear hunts.

Pittsburg   *North Country*

Pittsburg is unique, not so much in being the largest and north-ernmost town in New Hampshire, but in being a town that once was also an independent nation (see *Indian Stream*). But, while Pittsburg's history and geography may be unique, its name is not. Pittsfield, New Hampshire, and all the other Pittsburgs in the U.S. are named after the same man, William Pitt (1708–78), the great English statesman and advocate of mild treatment for the American colonies.

Pleasant, Mount (4,761 feet)
Mount Washington, Southern Ridges

See *Mount Eisenhower*.

Pleasant River   *Speckled Mountain Region*

Names such as this are common throughout the U.S., often re-flecting more of the namers' spirits and the circumstances of the nam-ing than any intrinsic characteristics of the feature itself.

Pliny Range, Mountain (3,605 feet)   *North Country*

Pliny, as every Latin student knows, was a first-century Roman poet, and like so many eponymous figures in the White Mountains, a great student of botany. It is said the name was given to this range in the southern part of the Kilkenny Basin by a local gentleman ac-quainted with classical history. Pliny Mountain, 3,605 feet, is in the southwest part of the range; the highest summit is *Mount Waumbek*, 4,005 feet.

Pond Brook; Pond Brook Falls   *North Country*

The brook's name may be prosaic—derived from this tributary of *Nash Stream* being formed from the outflow of Whitcomb and Trio Ponds—but the waterfall on it is a scenic delight.

Pondicherry Notch   *North Country*

Around 1907 John Anderson of the Mount Crawford House suggested this name for the notch between *Mount Deception* and *Cherry Mountain* because Pondicherry was the original name for Cherry Mountain (see entry). The name Pondicherry is quite old; it appeared on the charter map of *Bretton Woods,* granted in 1772, and in the journal of Dr. Jeremy Belknap, who toured the region in 1784. But of the name's origin little is known. It is possible the name describes a pond around which cherries grew, and it has also been suggested that the name was given by French explorers who were recalling Pondicherry, capital of French India and the site of frequent struggles between the French and the British.

Pondicherry Wildlife Refuge   *North Country*

Designated a National Natural Landmark, this 300-acre tract of bog and pond takes its name from an old name, of obscure origin, for *Cherry Pond* and *Cherry Mountain* (see entry). It includes Big Cherry Pond and Little Cherry Pond. *Pondicherry Notch* is nearby.

Pond of Safety   *North Country*

James Rider, Benjamin Hicks, William Danforth, and Lazarus Homes were soldiers in the Continental Army who had been captured by the British and later paroled. American officers believed the soldiers' parole papers were spurious, and they ordered the men back into the ranks. The four refused to break their word to the British and to bear arms against them, so they returned to their native town of *Jefferson* in the White Mountains. They were branded as deserters by the Army, so they fled to this wilderness pond in the easterly section of *Randolph* (then called Durand) where they lived for the next three years until the war was over. They then returned to Jefferson where they became prominent and respected citizens. In 1826 they were exonerated of the desertion charge, and their names were added to the Army's pension lists.

Pontook Reservoir North Country

The name Pontook is an abbreviation of the Abenaki word "pontoocook," meaning "falls in the river," and indeed there are falls just below these wetlands on the *Androscoggin River* above *Berlin*.

Potato Hill Moosilauke Region

Early settlers grew California potatoes on this hill near *Elbow Pond* in *Woodstock* and sold them to Elder Rope's Starch Mill on Glover Brook.

Presidential Range Mount Washington, Southern Ridges

On July 31, 1820, a party of seven men ascended *Mount Washington* for the stated purpose of naming the high peaks. The seven were Adino N. Brackett, John W. Weeks, Gen. John Wilson, Charles J. Stuart, Noyes S. Dennison, Samuel A. Pearson—all of *Lancaster*—and the mapmaker Philip Carrigain, then New Hampshire secretary of state. They were guided in their journey by Ethan Allen Crawford.

Mount Washington had already received its name, so they decided to christen the adjacent peaks for the four subsequent presidents—John Adams, Thomas Jefferson, James Madison, and James Monroe, who was in office at the time. The naming was a momentous event, and the namers had brought with them plenty of "O-be-joyful" so that proper toasts could be drunk. Then, running out of presidents, they christened *Mount Franklin* for Benjamin Franklin, and the next peak to the southwest they called Mount Pleasant (now *Mount Eisenhower*), a name it facetiously has been suggested was inspired by the O-be-joyful.

Since then the names of other presidents have been added to the Presidential Range—John Quincy Adams, Franklin Pierce, and most recently Dwight David Eisenhower. Other presidents having their names on peaks in the White Mountains, though not in the Presidential Range, are Abraham Lincoln, James A. Garfield, Grover Cleveland, and Calvin Coolidge.

Presidential Range–Dry River Wilderness Area
Mount Washington, Southern Ridges

This 27,380-acre USFS wilderness area was designated in 1975 and named, like the other WMNF wilderness areas, for prominent

natural features within its boundaries. An additional 7,000 acres were added in 1984.

Profile Lake   *Cannon, Kinsman*

It is said the Indians rarely visited this lake because they feared the reflection of the stern visage above. Early settlers called the pond Ferrin Pond, after the Ferrin family who helped build a road through *Franconia Notch*. It also was called Old Man's Washbowl, for the *Old Man of the Mountain*. Today the pond is called Profile Lake, corresponding to Profile Mountain above it.

Profile Mountain (4,077 feet)   *Cannon, Kinsman*

See *Cannon Mountain*.

Prospect, Mount (2,059 feet)   *North Country*

Early residents of Lancaster called this knob south of the village Mount Prospect because of the extended views from its top. John Wingate Weeks (1860–1920), U.S. secretary of war during President Harding's administration, built a summer home atop the mountain, and the family later gave the home and the mountain to New Hampshire to become *Weeks State Park*. John W. Weeks was largely responsible for the creation of the WMNF.

Pulpit Rock   *Carter, Baldface Ranges*

On *Carter Dome*'s east side is a huge boulder named Pulpit Rock because it is partly detached from the cliff and is evocative of a pulpit.

Quimbys Pillow *Carter, Baldface Ranges*   127

In 1879 Prof. E. T. Quimby occupied the summit of *Mount Moriah* as one of the stations of the U.S. Coast and Geodetic Survey; this boulder, weighing about 500 pounds and three-quarters of a mile from the summit, was jocularly named for him.

Randolph (town), Path; Mount (3,070 feet)

Northern Peaks, Great Gulf

The town of Randolph originally was chartered in 1772 as Durand, for John Durand, an English business associate of Gov. Benning Wentworth. The name was changed to Randolph in 1824 by Gov. Levi Woodbury to honor his friend Congressman John Randolph of Virginia (1773–1833). Known as John Randolph of Roanoke, he was a descendant of Pocahontas. He later became a U.S. senator and a leading advocate of state's rights.

The Randolph Path, which goes from Dolly Copp Road over the slopes of *Mounts Madison* and *Adams* to join the *Gulfside Trail* in *Edmands Col*, was built by the famous White Mountains trailmaker J. Rayner Edmands. He constructed the portion above timberline in 1893 and the section below timberline in 1897–99. Parts of the trail were reconstructed in 1978 in honor of Christopher Goetze, active member of the Randolph Mountain Club and editor of the AMC's journal, *Appalachia*.

Mount Randolph, two miles northwest of the village and named for it, originally was called Black Mountain, but it appeared on an 1858 map under its present name.

Rattlesnake Mountain (general)

New Hampshire does have rattlesnakes—though they are rare—and an incident involving one would have been memorable. Consequently New Hampshire has several Rattlesnake Mountains; GNIS lists five, as well as seven Rattlesnake Hills. In the White Mountains, Rattlesnake Mountains are found as follows:

Rattlesnake Mountain (1,550 feet) *Carter, Baldface Ranges*

Peak in the Green Hills east of North Conway. See *Rattlesnake Mountain (general)*.

Rattlesnake Mountain *Carter, Baldface Ranges*

Small summit northwest of Kezar Lake; Rattlesnake Brook flows to the west. See *Rattlesnake Mountain (general)*.

Rattlesnake Mountain *Carter, Baldface Ranges*

Small summit northeast of Keewaydin Lake. See *Rattlesnake Mountain (general)*.

Rattlesnake Mountain (1,594 feet) *Moosilauke Region*
Rattlesnake Mountain, Upper (2,160 feet)

Two summits west of Rumney. See *Rattlesnake Mountain (general)*.

Raymond Cataract, Path
Mount Washington, Southern Ridges

In 1859 Maj. Curtis B. Raymond, a veteran mountaineer, led an exploring party to these falls, and his companions named them in his honor. Four years later Major Raymond blazed a path nearby to connect the Carriage Road with the *Tuckerman Ravine* Path. He completed the path that now bears his name in 1879, and he maintained it until his death in 1893, when his widow generously continued to maintain it.

Redstone *Carter, Baldface Ranges*

In 1886 quarry operations were begun at this site between *Conway* and North Conway, the object being the red granite located here. A small industrial settlement grew up, taking its name from the stone's color.

Resolution, Mount (3,428 feet)
Mount Washington, Southern Ridges

Nathaniel T. P. Davis was son-in-law of Abel Crawford and manager of the Mount Crawford House in *Crawford Notch* (see *Davis*

Brook, Path; Mount). In 1845 he set about building the third bridle path to *Mount Washington,* but he got only as far as this mountain before he gave up, discouraged, something easily understandable given the rugged terrain. Later, however, and with renewed determination and "resolution," he tried again and this time succeeded, so Dr. Samuel Bemis, a friend and neighbor, suggested this name for the mountain where Davis started the second time.

Ridge of the Caps   *Northern Peaks, Great Gulf*

This ridge on *Mount Jefferson*'s west side takes its name from prominent rock formations called the Caps, ranging in elevation from 4,422 feet to 4,830 feet. Formations akin to these on Mount Jefferson's northwest ridge are called Castles; see *Castellated Ridge.* The trail along the Ridge of the Caps, connecting *Jefferson Notch* with the *Appalachian Trail,* is called the Caps Ridge Trail.

Riley Mountain (approx. 2,300 feet)   *Mahoosuc Range Area*

This mountain between the Bull Branch of the *Sunday River* and Miles Notch Brook probably takes its name, like nearby Riley Hill and Riley Township in Maine, for Luke Riley and family, early settlers of Newry.

Ripley Falls   *Franconia, Twin, Willey Ranges*

In 1858 an old fisherman reported to Henry Wheelock Ripley of North Conway that he had seen a wonderful cascade on what was then called Cow Brook, at the southern end of *Crawford Notch.* Ripley and a friend, a Mr. Porter of New York, followed up on the report, which they discovered to be true. (It has been speculated that this "old fisherman" might have been Abel Crawford, who Moses F. Sweetser said discovered the falls earlier, "while out on snowshoes, trapping sable.") In 1859 Rev. Thomas Starr King reported the Ripley-Porter discovery and reported as well that they had called the waterfall Sylvan-Glade Cataract, and called another waterfall further upstream Sparkling Cascade. Reverend King proposed naming the lower waterfall for Ripley, and he also proposed renaming Cow Brook, calling it instead *Avalanche Brook* because it flows near the track of the landslide that wiped out the Willey family in 1826.

Only a few persons have ever equaled Ripley's familiarity with and love for the White Mountains. Born in 1828 in Fryeburg, Maine, he began visiting the White Mountains when he was seven; the summer of 1889 was his fifty-third consecutive visit to the White Mountains, and he had climbed *Mount Washington,* in summer and in winter, eighty-five times. He was well known for his conversation and writings about the White Mountains, and he prepared for publication the second edition of Lucy Crawford's *History of the White Mountains* in 1883.

Riverton North Country

Named doubtless for being on the *Israel River* in *Jefferson,* this tiny settlement was the birthplace of Thaddeas Lowe (1832–1913), an aeronautic scientist and early student of the atmosphere.

Rocky Branch; Rocky Branch Ridge
Mount Washington, Southern Ridges

The Rocky Branch of the *Saco River* heads south of Slide Peak and flows south in the valley separating *Montalban Ridge* and Rocky Branch Ridge to join the Saco River west of *Glen.* Features named Rocky are common throughout the U.S., the best known being the Rocky Mountains.

Rocky Gorge *Chocorua, East Sandwich*

Nine miles west of *Conway* on the *Swift River* is this waterfall also known as Upper Falls; Lower Falls are two miles further east.

Rogers Ledge *North Country*

The present name of this rock outcropping in the Kilkenny Basin is the result of a crusade. The ledge previously had been known as Nigger Nose, but in 1955 the Right Rev. Robert McConnell Hatch, Bishop of the Episcopal Diocese of Western Massachusetts and a longtime summer resident of *Randolph,* decided it should be changed. He proposed the name Rogers Ledge to honor Maj. Robert Rogers, who led the famous Rogers Rangers during the French and Indian Wars. Hatch pointed out that though Major Rogers ended the Indian raids in the North Country and made the region safe for settlement, no geographical feature here was named for him.

Hatch discovered that Edward DeCourcy, a respected New Hampshire weekly newspaper editor, had written an editorial suggesting that the name Nigger Nose be changed, and the two worked together to accomplish this. Their cause was joined by the Automobile Legal

Association., which in 1964 wrote to U.S. Secretary of the Interior Stewart Udall that the name Nigger Nose "offends the sensibilities of all right-thinking people." The association advocated naming the ledge after the late President Kennedy.

Their efforts were successful—though Major Rogers won out over President Kennedy—and in 1964 the USBGN formally decreed that henceforth the outcrop would be Rogers Ledge.

Rollins Trail
Chocorua, East Sandwich

Dr. William H. Rollins, who had a summer home in Tamworth for many years, in 1899 paid for the construction of this path connecting *Mounts Passaconaway* and *Whiteface.*

Rosebrook Mountains, Mountain (3,007 feet)
Franconia, Twin, Willey Ranges

Capt. Eleazer Rosebrook was an early guide and settler in the White Mountains. Born in Grafton, Massachusetts, in 1747, he moved north, living first in Lunenburg, Vermont, then *Colebrook,* New Hampshire, and then Guildhall, Vermont. In 1790 Captain Rosebrook's daughter, Hannah, married Abel Crawford, and in 1792 he followed his son-in-law in settling the site later known as *Fabyan.* (Abel Crawford moved down the road twelve miles.) In 1803 the New Hampshire legislature authorized the construction of a turnpike through *Crawford Notch,* and, as travel and business increased, Captain Rosebrook built a large two-story dwelling abutting a mound known as Giants Grave. This inn built by Captain Rosebrook has been called the first summer hotel in the White Mountains; he called it the "Old Red Tavern." In 1817 Captain Rosebrook gave his inn to his grandson Ethan Allen Crawford, who along with Ethan's future bride, Lucy, nursed their grandfather during his final illness; Captain Rosebrook died at his farm that year.

The mountains are listed as Rosebrook Mountains in GNIS, though they often appear as the Rosebrook Range; they are an extension of the *Willey* Range and include Mounts Echo (3,084 feet), Rosebrook (3,007 feet), *Oscar* (2,748 feet), and *Stickney* (approximately 3,065 feet).

Round Mountain (3,890 feet)
North Country

Its appearance from the west likely is responsible for the name of this peak in the *Pliny Range.*

Royce Mountain, West (3,202 feet)

Carter, Baldface Ranges

Royce Mountain, East (3,115 feet)

Capt. Vere Royce was a soldier and surveyor and at one time served as surveyor-general of the Province of New Hampshire. He made charter maps for many White Mountains towns, including *Chatham, Bartlett,* and *Bretton Woods.* In 1769 he was granted 2,000 acres near the *Saco River* between *Glen* and Bartlett; the land was given for his services "during the late war in North America," but Captain Royce never settled here. This peak west of *Evans Notch* and nearby East Royce were named for him. The name Royse Mountain appeared on Samuel Holland's 1784 map.

R

133

Rump Mountain (3,647 feet) *North Country*

This remote Maine mountain, just east of the New Hampshire line, once was called Mount Carmel, but this likely was a mistaken interpretation of the name Camels Rump, from its appearance from the southwest.

Sabbaday Brook, Falls   *Chocorua, East Sandwich*

According to tradition, early settlers on their way to new homes paused on the Sabbath Day near this brook north of *Mount Tripyramid*. They pondered the likely conditions at their destination, reconsidered their venture—and turned around. Moses F. Sweetser, in his 1887 guidebook, labeled the falls Church Falls on Sabbaday Brook, to honor Frederick Edwin Church, a well-known landscape painter (see *Church Ponds*), but the name didn't stick.

Sable Mountain (3,504 feet)   *Carter, Baldface Ranges*

The name of this summit in northwestern *Chatham* appeared on Philip Carrigain's 1816 map. The name could refer to the peak being dark in color. Or more likely it could refer to the minklike animal known as sable (*Mustela Americana*), more commonly known as pine marten. Or it could refer to something else entirely; no information has been found as to the origin of this name.

Sachem Peak (2,860 feet)   *Waterville Valley Region*

"Sachem" meant "chief" to the Indians of the Northeast; this peak was named by Prof. C. E. Fay because it is the highest peak on *Acteon Ridge*.

Saco Lake, River   *Mount Washington, Southern Ridges*

"Saco" in the Abenaki language meant "flowing out, outlet," a name possibly attached originally to tiny Saco Lake in *Crawford Notch* and then later, by extension, to the stream flowing out of it.

The Saco River East Fork heads on the west side of *South Baldface* and flows southwest, becoming the East Branch, to join the main Saco River near Lower *Bartlett.*

Saddleback Mountain (3,812 feet)   *Mahoosuc Range Area*

The present name of this mountain east of *Grafton Notch* comes from its shape; it also has been called Bear River Whitecap and, more commonly, Baldpate.

Salmacis Falls   *Northern Peaks, Great Gulf*

On July 21, 1879, according to a contemporary account in *Among the Clouds,* some visitors from *Randolph* named these falls on *Snyder Brook* for the wood nymph, Salmacis. In classical mythology, however, Salmacis was a fountain in Caria that rendered effeminate all who bathed in it, and it was in this fountain that Hermaphroditus underwent a sex change.

Salmon Hole Brook   *Cannon, Kinsman*

On the *Ammonoosuc River* 2.5 miles south of *Lisbon* is a deep hole where salmon weighing as much as twenty-five pounds once were caught. The Indians salted them for the winter, and the white settlers also fed on them until industrial mills upstream polluted the water, destroying the fishery.

Sandwich (town), Mountain (3,993 feet)
Waterville Valley Region

Sandwich Range
Waterville Valley Region, Chocorua, East Sandwich

Sandwich Mountain, located south of *Waterville Valley,* and the Sandwich Range, took their name from the town of Sandwich still further south. The town was chartered in 1763 by Gov. Benning Wentworth, who named it to honor John Montagu (1718–92), fourth Earl of Sandwich, influential with King George II and George III. (Yes, the sandwich made with slices of bread also owes its name to him.) When first laid out, the New Hampshire town had so many "inaccessible mountains and shelves of rock" it was thought to be uninhabitable; seventeen peaks are listed in the town. Sandwich Mountain, highest of these, had been called Sandwich Dome, as well as Black Mountain, but in 1910 the USBGN approved the name Sandwich Mountain and put the name Black Mountain on a subsidiary summit one mile southwest.

Sandwich Range Wilderness Area *Waterville Valley Region*

This 25,000-acre USFS wilderness area was designated in 1984 and named for the mountains it includes.

Sanguinary Mountain (2,748 feet) *North Country*

"Sanguinarius" in Latin means "blood-colored"; this peak forming the north flank of *Dixville Notch* was named for the brilliant blood-red color of its rocks at sunset.

Sargent Brook, Mountain (approx. 2,350 feet)
Mahoosuc Range Area

Reuben Sargent and his family were settlers in this area by 1842.

Sargent Cliff, Path *North Country*

Dr. George A. Sargent, a physician, was among the regular summer visitors to *Randolph*; he first came in 1882 and returned until his death in 1932. This cliff in *Ice Gulch* on *Mount Crescent* and the path connecting Durand Road with Lookout Ledge both bear his name.

Sargents Purchase *Mount Washington, Southern Ridges*

In 1831, these lands that include the summit of *Mount Washington,* as well as *Lakes of the Clouds, Tuckerman Ravine,* and *Mount Monroe,* were purchased for $300 by a group of men among whom was Jacob Sargent of Thornton.

Saunders, Mount (3,120 feet) *Carrigain, Moat Regions*

The Saunders family for generations owned and managed timberlands in *Livermore,* and one of its members, Charles C. Saunders of Lawrence, Massachusetts, gained recognition as an early promoter of scientific forestry, as well as being an AMC charter member. Local people had long called this mountain between *Mount Nancy* and Livermore Station Mount Saunders, and the name was formally approved by the AMC Committee on Nomenclature in 1915. The name honors the Hon. Daniel Saunders, who died at Lawrence in 1917, at the age of ninety-four.

Savage Mountain (3,503 feet)   *North Country*

Raymond Aaron Savage was a long-time *Stratford* fire chief and selectman who was brutally murdered in 1976 at the age of 70. The murder was later solved, and shortly after Savage's death his son, Wiliam, suggested to the USBGN that a 3,503-foot peak just south of *Goback Mountain* in Stratford be named for him, for Savage loved to hunt near the mountain. In January 1979, the USBGN granted the request.

Sawyer Pond, River, Rock   *Carrigain, Moat Regions*

Benjamin Sawyer was an early settler and explorer in the White Mountains who, along with Timothy Nash (see *Nash and Sawyers Location*), achieved a place in history by helping prove that men and horses could travel through *Crawford Notch*. The two accomplished their goal only with great difficulty, and several times they had to lower a horse down rock faces with ropes. Finally, says tradition, just as they had overcome their last obstacle, they halted and celebrated by breaking a bottle—presumably of rum—on Sawyer Rock in commemoration of their victory. Sawyer River heads southwest of *Mount Hancock* and flows east to join the *Saco River* just northeast of Sawyer Rock. Sawyer Pond, once called Bemis Lake, and Little Sawyer Pond, southwest of Sawyer Rock, are the focus for the WMNF Sawyer Pond Scenic Area.

Scar Ridge   *Waterville Valley Region*

Running northwest from *Mount Osceola*, this ridge was named in 1876 by Prof. F. W. Clarke and Gaetano Lanza, who made an early ascent of it. The name is derived from the ridge having recently been scarred by landslides at the time of the naming.

The Scaur   *Waterville Valley Region*

Scaur is just a variant spelling of "scar." The Scaur is a rock outlook between *Mad River* and Slide Brook.

Screw Auger Falls
Waterville Valley Region

On the Bear River, southwest of Grafton Notch, rushing water has worn holes into the river's rock bed. So regular are some of the holes that they appear to have been made with an auger, hence the name.

Sebosis Brook
Mount Washington, Southern Ridges

In 1936 the USBGN recognized this as the approved name for this tributary of Crawford Brook. Sebosis Brook had also been called Clinton Brook, because it heads on the slopes of the mountain previously known as Mount Clinton, now *Mount Pierce*. The meaning of the brook's present name is unknown.

Second College Grant
North Country

This tract of uninhabited forest land in the state's far north was Gov. Benning Wentworth's second choice—hence the name—as a site for Dartmouth College. His first choice was the present town of *Landaff*, and his third was Hanover. Six square miles of land here were granted officially to the college in 1807, and Dartmouth enjoyed considerable revenue from subsequent sales of real estate and timber. An act of the legislature in 1919 authorized the continued use of the name Second College Grant in the list of state towns and gave to the college whatever state money and resources Second College Grant might be allocated.

Second Connecticut Lake
North Country

See *Connecticut Lakes*.

Shaw, Mount (2,566 feet)
Carter, Baldface Ranges

Lemuel Shaw (1781–1861) was a member of Dr. Jacob Bigelow's 1816 botanical expedition to the White Mountains, the first to explore *Mount Washington* for scientific knowledge. Shaw, the son of a Congregational minister, was assistant editor of a Boston newspaper, studied law, and drafted the Boston City charter. In 1830 he became chief justice of the Massachusetts Supreme Court. This peak northeast of *Mount Kearsarge North* was named for him.

Shehadi, Camp
Waterville Valley Region

In 1899 *Wonalancet* Outdoor Club used the proceeds from a lecture to build the predecessor to this camp located one-fifth mile from the summit of *Mount Whiteface*. The lecturer was one Shehadi Abdullah Shehadi. (The original shelter was replaced in 1930.)

Shelburne
Mahoosuc Range Area

In 1769 this town straddling the *Androscoggin River* was named for William Petty Fitzmaurice (1737–1805), Earl of Shelburne. He was one of the American colonies' staunchest friends in Parliament in the days before the American Revolution.

Shelburne Moriah Mountain (3,735 feet)
Carter, Baldface Ranges

See *Mount Moriah*.

Sherman Adams Summit Building
Mount Washington, Southern Ridges

Ethan Allen Crawford in the 1820s constructed the first shelter atop *Mount Washington*—a tent, which was shortlived. Between 1841 and 1844 a crude log cabin, twelve feet square, was built on the summit; its builder and fate are unknown. Finally, in 1852, the Summit House, the first structure to provide more than temporary shelter, was built. It was followed in 1853 by the *Tip Top House* and in 1872–73 by the Second Summit House. The present Sherman Adams summit building, dedicated in 1980, honors Sherman Adams —lumber company executive, U.S. represenative, governor, special assistant to President Eisenhower, AMC and SPNHF member, and president of Loon Mountain Corporation—long known for his deep love of and involvement in the White Mountains.

Shoal Pond
Franconia, Twin, Willey Ranges

Shoal refers to the pond's shallowness. Shoal Pond Brook heads here and runs south into the East Branch of the *Pemigewasset River*.

Short Line Trail
Northern Peaks, Great Gulf

The well-known White Mountains trailmaker J. Rayner Edmands in 1899–1901 constructed this 1.9-mile path to connect the *Air Line Trail* with the *King Ravine Trail*. It was named for its relatively short length.

Silver Cascade
Mount Washington, Southern Ridges

On the *Mount Jackson*'s west side, flowing into the *Saco River,* is a series of falls known as Silver Cascade. The name has been in general use since the 1850s when Rev. Thomas Starr King visited the area. Before that the falls were known as the Second Flume, probably because they are south of Flume Cascade (see *The Flume*).

Silver Spring, Mount (2,995 feet)
Carrigain, Moat Regions

See *Bartlett Haystack.*

Six Husbands Trail
Northern Peaks, Great Gulf

Weetamoo was a female Indian chief (see *Weetamoo*) who, according to tradition, had six husbands in succession. John Greenleaf Whittier used her name for the heroine of his poem "The Bridal of Pennacook," and, when the *Great Gulf* Trail was blazed in 1908, beautiful *Weetamoo Fall* below *Spaulding Lake* was named for her. The next year, the section of the trail connecting the Great Gulf with the *Gulfside Trail* was constructed, and it was named for Weetamoo's six husbands; the name later was applied to the entire trail. The first of her husbands was Wamsutta, whose name is on the *Wamsutta Trail,* also in the Great Gulf.

Skookumchuck Brook
Franconia, Twin, Willey Ranges

This name is analogous to a glacial "erratic," appearing out of context far from its original place of origin. The name is derived from jargon of the Chinook Indians of the Pacific Northwest, and it means "dashing water" or "rapids." The brook heads on the north side of *Garfield Ridge* and flows northwest.

Sleeper Ridge
Waterville Valley Region

As the AMC guide puts it: "Though this ridge could have been named quite aptly for the sleepy appearance of its two rounded, rather gently sloping domes [West Peak, 3,870 feet, and East Peak, 3,850 feet], it is actually named for Katherine Sleeper Walden, a civic-minded local innkeeper whose efforts in trail-building (she founded the Wonalancet Outdoor Club), conservation, and public improvements were so energetic and pervasive that she earned the sobriquet of 'matriarch of Wonalancet and the WODC' and is memorialized by two natural features (Sleeper Ridge and *Mount Katherine*) and two trails (the Sleeper and *Walden* trails)."

Slope Mountain (2,008 feet)   *Carter, Baldface Ranges*

The derivation of the name of this mountain northwest of *Chatham* is unknown, but it appeared as Sloop Mountain on Samuel Holland's map of 1784.

Snow Arch   *Mount Washington, Southern Ridges*

Hikers have been fascinated by this natural arch of snow in *Tuckerman Ravine* at least since 1829, when Ethan Allen Crawford guided a party of botanists into the region. During the winter, snow blows over the steep walls of the ravine and accumulates below, sometimes reaching depths of 200 to 300 feet. Meltwater from the snow and ice sometimes erodes the snow into the shape of an arch. These arches are not formed every year, but when they are they can be impressive; one was 40 feet high, 84 feet wide, and 255 feet long.

Snows Brook, Mountain (approx. 3,000 feet)
Waterville Valley Region

William Snow was an early settler of *Waterville Valley* who around 1830 built his cabin near this mountain. The brook, south of the mountain, flows west to Waterville Valley.

Snyder Brook   *Northern Peaks, Great Gulf*

In 1875 this brook heading at Star Lake between *Mounts Madison* and Quincy *Adams* was named by the White Mountains trailmaker William G. Nowell, supposedly for the little dog of Charles E. Lowe, another trailmaker. The brook has been known as Salmacis Brook, but following a 1936 USBGN decision only *Salmacis Falls* has this name.

South Kinsman (4,358 feet)   *Cannon, Kinsman*

See *Mount Kinsman.*

South Pond   *North Country*

South Pond, the site of a state park in *Stark,* was once the geographical counterpart of nearby North Pond, which has since been rechristened *Christine Lake.*

Spaulding Lake   *Northern Peaks, Great Gulf*

Located at the head of the *Great Gulf,* this tiny lake was named for John H. Spaulding, author of *Historical Relics of the White Mountains,* first published in 1855, and a manager of the *Tip Top House* on *Mount Washington.* Spaulding was a hardy explorer of the White Mountains. In 1853 he first visited the lake later named for him; in February 1862 Spaulding with two companions made the first recorded overnight stay on the summit of Mount Washington in the winter. In 1891, on his seventieth birthday, he once again climbed Mount Washington.

Spaulding Spring   *Northern Peaks, Great Gulf*

Near *Edmands Col,* between *Mounts Jefferson* and *Adams,* is a reliable spring discovered in 1875 by Rev. Henry G. Spaulding of Brookline, Massachusetts, and named for him by his companions, Charles G. Lowe and Dr. William G. Nowell.

Speckled Mountain (2,906 feet)   *Speckled Mountain Region*

At least three mountains in Maine—and none in New Hampshire—have this name, which has been explained as coming from their scattered, open ledges but also from their varied vegetation, especially when viewed in the fall. See also *Old Speck.*

Sphinx Col, Trail   *Northern Peaks, Great Gulf*

This trail connecting the *Great Gulf* Trail with the *Gulfside Trail* at Sphinx Col between *Mounts Jefferson* and *Clay* takes its name from the profile of a rock formation as viewed from just below the meadow where water is found.

Spruce Mountain (2,272 feet)   *Carter, Baldface Ranges*
Spruce Mountain (3,065 feet)   *North Country*

GNIS lists 14 New Hampshire features named for spruce, but only two mountains—both in the White Mountains.

Stairs Mountain (3,460 feet)
Mount Washington, Southern Ridges

To Dr. Samuel Bemis of *Harts Location,* two precipitous steplike ledges on this mountain's southeast slope reminded him of "giants' stairs," and he proposed both that name (see *Giant Stairs*) and the name Stairs Mountain. A third and similar cliff east of the main summit is sometimes called the Back Stair. Draining the ridge to the east are, from the north, Stairs Brook, Upper Stairs Brook, and Lower Stairs Brook.

Stalbird Brook *North Country*

In later life she was known to all in the town of *Jefferson* as Granny Stalbird, but when this hardy and determined woman first appeared in the White Mountains she was Deborah Vickers, a young maiden working as a cook on the baronial estate of Col. Joseph Whipple. She lived in Jefferson eighteen months before she saw another white woman, and she is said to have made the first maple syrup in the fledgling settlement. She also is credited with bringing the first Bible to town; she paid five dollars for the Bible, the equivalent of ten weeks' wages on the Whipple estate.

Colonel Whipple's reputation as a shrewd and parsimonious taskmaster has survived nearly 200 years. According to tradition, he once paid Deborah Vickers a year's wages in depreciated Continental currency, money he knew to be nearly valueless. When Deborah Vickers discovered she had been cheated, she confronted Colonel Whipple and so roundly and effectively upbraided him that he offered her any fifty acres in town not already sold—in addition to the payment she'd already received. She had some of this land cleared before she temporarily left the White Mountains for Portsmouth, where she married Richard Stalbird. She returned to her homestead the next spring and exchanged some of her rocky land for better acreage. She remained in Jefferson the rest of her long life.

In the town of *Shelburne* was a huge rock known as Stalbird Ledge. The rock was destroyed during railroad construction, but tradition has it that an aged woman named Stalbird once took refuge beneath the rock during a storm. The woman had to remain standing all night and until noon the following day, holding her horse's bridle. It is not known if the woman was Granny Stalbird of Jefferson, but the act would have been in character for her.

Stanton, Mount (1,748 feet)
Mount Washington, Southern Ridges

Probably named for a *Bartlett* family, this peak marks the beginning of *Montalban Ridge*. It formerly was known as Rattlesnake Mountain, one of many mountains having that name in New Hamp-

S

143

shire, but it appeared as Mount Stanton on Prof. Charles H. Hitch-cock's map of 1876.

Stark

When first granted in 1774, this town on the *Upper Ammonoosuc River* was called *Percy,* named like its neighbor, *Northumberland,* for Hugh Smithson, Earl Percy, and First Duke of Northumberland. In 1832 it was renamed to honor Gen. John Stark, hero of the battles of Bennington and Bunker Hill, native son of New Hampshire whose advice in a letter—"live free or die"—later became the state motto. The tiny settlement of Percy and the *Percy Peaks* in nearby Stratford preserve the original name.

Starr King (settlement); Mount (3,913 feet)
North Country

The White Mountains have probably never had a more passionate and prolific popularizer than Rev. Thomas Starr King. Born in 1824, he began visiting the region as a youth, and he later wrote in the Boston *Transcript* about his explorations. He became a Unitarian minister, and in 1859 his book *The White Hills: Their Legends, Landscapes, and Poetry* was published. This book was very popular at the time, and in it he rhapsodized about the natural beauties of the White Mountains. He later moved to San Francisco, where he became an equally enthusiastic explorer of the mountains there, and a peak in Yosemite National Park is named for him. In the White Mountains, Mount Starr King in the *Pliny Range* and *King Ravine* on *Mount Adams* are named for him, as well as the hamlet on U.S. Route 2 one mile northwest of Jefferson Highlands. The peak has been called Starr King Mountain, but the form approved by the USBGN in 1959 is Mount Starr King.

Step Falls
Mahoosuc Range Area

Located a half-mile up Wight Brook from its confluence with Bear River, northwest of Newry, Maine, Step Falls takes its name from a series of steplike ledges. The falls are on a twenty-four-acre preserve of The Nature Conservancy.

Stewartstown
North Country

When Gov. John Wentworth first granted this town on the upper *Connecticut River,* he intended it to be developed by a group of men who included Sir George Colebrook and Sir James Cockburn, both connected with the British East India Company, and Sir John Stuart, Lord Bute, who had influence with the new king, George III. The group honored Lord Bute by naming their 6,000-acre holding Stuart. When the town was incorporated in 1799 after the Revolution, it was called Stewartstown, the name having reverted to the original Scottish form.

Stickney, Mount (3,070 feet) *Franconia, Twin, Willey Ranges*

Ironic it is that such an inconspicuous mountain as this should be named for the builder of such a magnificent edifice as the Mount Washington Hotel. Joseph Stickney was a New Hampshire native and for many years the owner of the Mount Pleasant House. He built the Mount Washington Hotel at *Bretton Woods* in 1901–1902. Guests of the Mount Pleasant House in 1878 called the mountain Ammonoosuc, for the nearby river, but the name never came into general use.

Stinson Lake, Mountain (2,870 feet) *Moosilauke Region*

In April 1752 a hunting parting consisting of David Stinson of Londonderry, Amos Eastman, and John Stark were attacked by Indians. According to tradition, Stinson and Eastman were killed and scalped on the shore of this lake near Rumney, while Stark was captured and taken to Canada. He later was ransomed and went on to become a hero in the Revolutionary War. The name Stinson Mountain first appeared on Philip Carrigain's 1816 map.

Stowe Mountain (approx. 2,300 feet) *Mahoosuc Range Area*

This southern extension of *Sunday River Whitecap* takes its name from the Stowe family, who lived here.

Stratford *North Country*

If this town were named Stratford-on-Connecticut, the name would be in keeping with its origins. Most if not all the Stratfords in the U.S.—and they also exist in Connecticut, New Jersey, Texas, Virginia, and Wisconsin—ultimately owe their names to Stratford-on-Avon, home of William Shakespeare.

New Hampshire's Stratford was originally granted as Woodbury in 1762, named because many of its grantees came from Woodbury,

Connecticut. Totalling 48,063 acres, the grant was one of the largest ever made in New Hampshire, but, because of Indian danger, few grantees ever claimed their lands. In 1773 Gov. John Wentworth regranted the land, this time under the name of Stratford, but the reason was the same: many settlers were from a town in Connecticut, Stratford, adjacent to Woodbury.

Streeter Pond   *Connecticut Region*

Located south of *Littleton* in the town of *Lisbon,* this pond was named for Ebenezer Streeter, the first settler in its vicinity.

Success   *Mahoosuc Range Area*

In the early 1770s, when relations between the colonies and England were deteriorating, some persons, such as Gov. John Wentworth, looked for signs of a more conciliatory attitude toward America. Thus, when word came in 1773 that the hated Stamp Act had been repealed, bells were rung, cannons were fired, and sermons were preached with titles like "Good news from a far country." Governor Wentworth was so elated by the news that he named an island on his Wolfeboro estate Stamp Act Island. Success was granted in 1773, and it is believed the name came from the Stamp Act repeal or possibly the refusal of the colonists to allow British tea to be imported into Boston, a refusal many colonists viewed as a "success."

Success, Mount (3,590 feet)   *Mahoosuc Range Area*

This peak just west of the New Hampshire-Maine border takes its name from the unincorporated town in which it is located. The mountain has mistakenly been called *Mount Ingalls,* a name properly applied to a peak about two miles to the south in the range, the present location of both names having been established by a 1936 USBGN decision.

Sugar Hill   *Cannon, Kinsman*

New Hampshire has forty-seven towns that originally were part of other towns, and Sugar Hill is the most recent. It was separated from the town of *Lisbon* in 1962 after much litigation. Its name comes a large grove of sugar maple trees. GNIS lists nine summits or ridges in New Hampshire named Sugar Hill.

Sugarloaf (general)

Soon after the sugar trade began in the seventeenth century, sugar was marketed not in its familiar granulated form but in cones, called "loaves," created when hot, liquid sugar was poured into molds; grocers would break off pieces of these sugarloaves and sell them by the pound. The sugarloaf shape was as familiar and recognizable to people of the time as is the shape of an ice cream cone today, and nothing could have been more natural than for conical mountains shaped like sugarloaves to be named for them. Indeed, this was so common that the term no longer is just a confectioner's term but also a geographer's, and now people who never knew sugar came in loaves nonetheless know that a landform with a conical symmetrical shape is likely to be named Sugarloaf. New Hampshire has at least six Sugarloafs, one each in Alexandria, *Benton,* and *Stratford,* as well as three south of *Twin Mountain.* Even *Mount Washington* briefly was called Sugarloaf.

Sugarloaf (approx. 1,310 feet)   *Chocorua, East Sandwich*

Small conical summit one mile east of White Ledge, west of *Conway.* See *Sugarloaf (general).*

Sugarloaf, Middle (2,526 feet)
Franconia, Twin, Willey Ranges

Sugarloaf, North (approx. 2,290 feet)

Sugarloaf, South (3,023 feet)

Collectively known as the *Sugarloaves,* these three summits are aligned roughly north-south north of *Mount Hale.* They are especially conspicuous from the highway east of the village of *Twin Mountain.* See *Sugarloaf (general).*

Sugarloaf Mountain (1,495 feet)   *Carter, Baldface Ranges*

Northwest of Kezar Lake, in the Evergreen Valley Winter Sports Area. See *Sugarloaf (general).*

Sugarloaf Mountain (2,609 feet)   *Moosilauke Region*

Summit west of Long Pond. See *Sugarloaf (general).*

Sugarloaf Mountain   (3,701 feet)   *North Country*

This peak in *Stratford* is the highest Sugarloaf in the White Mountains. See *Sugarloaf (general)*.

Sugarloaf Mountain   (approx. 2,000 feet)
Speckled Mountain Region

Small summit southeast of *Evans Notch,* between the confluence of *Bickford Brook* and *Cold River.*

Sugar Mountain   (2,449 feet)   *North Country*

Like the state's numerous Sugar Hills, this summit southwest of *Berlin* likely was named for its sugar maples.

Sunday River, Sunday River Whitecap   (3,376 feet)
Mahoosuc Range Area

The Sunday River, heading on the eastern slopes of the *Mahoosuc Range* and flowing east to the *Androscoggin River,* is said to have been discovered on Sunday—hence the name. The peak is to the north of the river.

Surprise, Mount   (2,225 feet)   *Carter, Baldface Ranges*

How this spur of *Mount Moriah* got its name is obscure. A possible explanation is that the panoramic view from this minor peak does indeed come upon a hiker as a "surprise." The summit was cleared of trees in the mid-1800s by fire and wind. Another Mount Surprise, 947 feet, is located immediately east of *Intervale.*

Swazeytown   *Waterville Valley Region*

In 1842 a man named Eben Swazey made a little clearing in *Waterville Valley* and settled here. And, although Swazey left after ten years, the site has borne the name Swazeytown ever since—with one exception. Some loggers once had a camp and a dam here; they called the locality Crazytown.

Swift Diamond River   *North Country*

See *Diamond.*

Swift River   *Waterville Valley Region*

Paralleling the *Kancamagus Highway,* the Swift River heads on *Mount Kancamagus* and flows swiftly east down the mountain valley into the *Saco River* just north of *Conway.* The Penacook Indians, for whom the river valley was a favorite hunting ground, called the river "chataguay," meaning "the principal stream." The present descriptive name appeared on Jeremy Belknap's 1791 map.

Swiftwater   *Connecticut Region*

This village in the town of *Bath* likely derives its name from the settlement being on the *Wild Ammonoosuc River.* In the village are Swiftwater Falls.

S

Table Mountain (2,663 feet) *Carrigain, Moat Regions*

"Table" is a common descriptive metaphor for mountains with relatively flat tops, including this summit southwest of Big *Attitash*.

Table Rock *North Country*

No wider than a table—hence its name—this rock platform juts out from Mount Gloriette's north side in *Dixville Notch* and offers excellent views from its 700-foot height.

Tarleton, Lake *Moosilauke Region*

Col. William Tarleton, for whom this lake in *Piermont* was named, epitomized the patriotic enthusiasm of the Revolution. He fought in the Revolutionary War, was a delegate to the 1791 Constitutional Convention, was a presidential elector in 1804, and was a member of the New Hampshire Governor's Council in 1808. He had four sons, whom he named George Washington, Thomas Jefferson, Benjamin Franklin, and James Madison. Colonel Tarleton settled on the lake later named for him, where he kept a tavern.

Tecumseh, Mount (4,004 feet) *Waterville Valley Region*

Numerous explanations exist as to why this peak west of the village of *Waterville Valley* bears the name of an Indian chief who lived hundreds of miles away. (*Mount Osceola* north of Waterville Valley was named for a Seminole chief who lived even farther away). Tecumseh was a Shawnee (1768–1813) who joined his brother, Tenskwatawa, in trying to unite the Ohio region tribes. The effort failed, through no fault of Tecumseh's, so he joined the British during the War of 1812 and was killed in the Battle of the Thames.

New Hampsphire state geologist Charles H. Hitchcock once was told that Mount Tecumseh was named by E. J. Young, a *Campton* photographer whose stereos are the earliest extant photographs of Waterville Valley. Moses F. Sweetser, in his White Mountains guide, recorded as hearsay that the mountain was named by a Wisconsin tourist, who would have been more familiar with Chief Tecumseh. Nathaniel L. Goodrich, in his history of Waterville Valley, suggests Michigan might have been meant instead of Wisconsin. He also suggests that Mounts Tecumseh and Osceola both might have been named by E. J. Connable of Jackson, Michigan, who came to Waterville Valley in 1859.

Terrace Mountain (3,670 feet) *North Country*

This peak in the *Pliny Range* was named for its appearance from the west.

Third Connecticut Lake *North Country*

See *Connecticut Lakes.*

13 Falls *Franconia, Twin, Willey Ranges*

See *No. 13 Falls.*

Thompson and Meserves Purchase
Mount Washington, Southern Ridges

In 1835 this 12,000-acre tract containing the north slope of *Mount Washington* and the summits of *Mounts Adams, Jefferson,* and *Clay* was granted to Samuel W. Thompson of *Conway* and George P. Meserve of *Jackson.* They paid $500 for their grant.

Thompson Brook, Falls *Carter, Baldface Ranges*

Col. J. M. "Landlord" Thompson was the proprietor of the first *Glen House,* which opened in 1853, and he laid out many paths in the area. In 1869 he drowned in the *Peabody River.* Thompson Brook heads on *Wildcat* Ridge and flows west toward its confluence with the Peabody River; Thompson Falls is near the site of the hotel Thompson once called home.

Thoreau Falls
Franconia, Twin, Willey Ranges

Moses F. Sweetser in his White Mountains guide named these falls on the North Fork of the *Pemigewasset River* for the famous writer and naturalist Henry David Thoreau (1817–62), who visited the White Mountains and climbed *Mount Washington* in 1839 and again in 1858. He never saw the falls named for him.

Thorn Mountain (2,287 feet)
Carter, Baldface Ranges

On Dr. Jeremy Belknap's 1791 map, this peak east of *Jackson* appeared as Crotch Mountain, but on Philip Carrigain's 1816 map it appeared under its present name, which is thought to have been inspired by thorn-bearing shrubs on the mountain.

Thornton
Mooslauke Region

Located on the *Pemigewasset River,* this town was founded as one of the earliest attempts to settle the wilderness using almost exclusively families from a single area. The grant was made in 1763 by Gov. Benning Wentworth, and most of the families were of Scots-Irish descent. They included Dr. Matthew Thornton (1714–1803), a Londonderry physician who at the age of four had come with his family from the Scots settlement in Londonderry, Ireland. Dr. Thornton was granted land in northern New Hampshire as a reward for having served as a surgeon in the Pepperell Expedition of 1745 during which New England troops captured Louisbourg, Nova Scotia. Dr. Thornton went on to become one of three persons from New Hampshire to sign the Declaration of Independence. He also was a justice in the New Hampshire Superior Court, a speaker in the House of Representatives, a member of the state senate, a delegate to the Continental Congress, and first president—a position similar to governor—of New Hampshire following the Revolutionary War.

Three Sisters Ridge
Chocorua, East Sandwich

Mount Chocorua's northeast ridge has three knobs only slightly lower than the main summit, and from these comes the ridge's name. Middle Sister, the highest, is 3,330 feet.

Tin Mountain (2,025 feet)
Carter, Baldface Ranges

The first discovery of tin in the U.S. was said to have been made on this low summit east of *Jackson*. Mining of the mineral followed its discovery, but active operations have long since ceased.

Tinker Brook

North Country

Samuel B. Robbins was a traveling tinker in the mid-1800s who went from house to house throughout northern New Hampshire. An eccentric character, he was overly fond of fishing in this brook near *Berlin,* and he chased away any local boys he found fishing here, much to their indignation.

Tip Top House

Mount Washington, Southern Ridges

When the first *Mount Washington* Summit House was built in 1852, its success inspired the construction a year later of another guest facility, the Tip Top House. Samuel F. Spaulding was the owner, and his managers included his nephew, John H. Spaulding, for whom *Spaulding Lake* was named. The Tip Top House had walls of large rocks and a flat roof for an observation deck. From 1877–84, the Tip Top House housed the offices of *Among the Clouds,* the first daily newspaper to be published from a mountaintop. In 1915 fire destroyed the Tip Top House, but it soon was rebuilt to be used as a Summit House annex until 1968 when both had deteriorated until they no longer could accommodate guests.

Tom, Mount (4,047 feet)

Franconia, Twin, Willey Ranges

In 1876 New Hampshire state geologist Charles H. Hitchcock named this peak west of *Crawford Notch* for Thomas J. Crawford, a son of Abel Crawford and for many years proprietor of the Crawford House. Mount Tom Brook heads on this mountain's north slope and runs northwest to Zealand River.

Trident Pass

Mahoosuc Range Area

The juxtaposition of three small summits here gave this pass east of Cascade Mountain its name. It appears as Trident Col in the AMC guide.

Triple Falls

Northern Peaks, Great Gulf

As the name suggests, this feature on Town Line Brook, off the *Dolly Copp Campground,* is a series of three waterfalls, each with its own name, from lower to upper: Proteus, Erebus, and Evans. Proteus, explain the Bolnicks in *Waterfalls of the White Mountains,* "comes from a sea god in Homer's *Odyssey,* who changed form at will. The derivative term 'protean'—meaning exceedingly variable—aptly describes the way the falls change character in response to the rains. . . . A short climb brings you to the most striking of the three falls, named Erebus after the mysterious darkness through which souls passed on their descent to Hades in Greek mythology. . . . Evans Falls is just above Erebus. . . . The name presumably honors the non-mythical Captain John Evans, who worked on the first road through *Pinkham Notch* in 1774 and later commanded troops in the *Androscoggin* valley following Indian raids in 1781."

Tripoli Road   *Waterville Valley Region*

Using an old logging railroad grade on its western side, this road through Thornton Notch was built by the USFS to connect *Waterville Valley* with *Woodstock*. It was completed in 1934, and the USFS assuaged fears of Waterville Valley residents that the route would end their seclusion, by having the road bypass the town. The road owes its name to its Woodstock end originally having been opened for the Tripoli Mill in *Thornton*. Tripoli, a diatomaceous mineral having numerous industrial uses, was dredged from the bottom of East Pond.

Tripyramid, Mount (4,140 feet)   *Waterville Valley Region*

Three distinct summits—North Peak, 4,140 feet; Middle Peak, 4,110 feet; and South Peak, 4,090 feet—inspired the name of this mountain east of *Waterville Valley*. The name was suggested by Prof. Arnold Guyot of Princeton, who in 1860 published a map of the White Mountains. The mountain had at one time been known as Passaconaway before that name was applied to another mountain (see *Mount Passaconaway*).

Tuckerman Ravine   *Mount Washington, Southern Ridges*

Dr. Edward Tuckerman (1817–86) was a distinguished American botanist; from 1858 to his death he was a professor of botany at Amherst College. He first visited the White Mountains in 1837, staying with Abel Crawford, and for twenty years he explored the White Mountains searching for botanical specimens. It was said of him that "no portion of the region, however dark its glens or inaccessible its peaks, was untrodden by his footsteps." He named *Oakes Gulf* for William Oakes, another botanist, and among his contributions was categorizing the botanical life zones on the *Presidential Range*. This huge cirque on the south side of *Mount Washington* was named for him as early as 1848, first appearing on a map in 1858.

Tumbledown-Dick Mountain (1,740 feet)
Mahoosuc Range Area

Several explanations exist for the name of this steep cliff forming a spur of *Bear Mountain*, north of *Gilead*, Maine. One is that a blind horse named Dick once "tumbled down" here. Another says a shepherd named Dick fell from the mountain trying to rescue a sheep. Still another says an Indian—named Dick, of course—fell to his death one foggy night. But as the *Dictionary of Maine Place-names* says, "It is quite possibly just a fanciful name for a mountain that sometimes had slides."

Twin Mountain
Franconia, Twin, Willey Ranges

This village on the *Ammonoosuc River*, in the town of Carroll, takes its name from the prominent twin summits—to the south.

Twin Mountain, North (4,926 feet)
Franconia, Twin, Willey Ranges
Twin Mountain, South (4,769 feet)

Only about 150 feet separate the elevations of these nearly identical peaks midway between *Crawford* and *Franconia Notches*.

Twitchell Brook
Mahoosuc Range Area

This short brook, joining the *Androscoggin* from the north near *Gilead*, Maine, was named for Capt. Eleazer Twitchell, an early settler.

Tyler Notch, Mountain (approx. 2,150 feet)
Speckled Mountain Region

Southeast of *Gilead* are these features, named for the Tyler family, who lived in the area in 1880.

Umbagog, Lake *North Country*

To the Abenaki Indians who once inhabited northern New Hampshire, the name of this lake straddling the New Hampshire-Maine border meant "clear lake" or "clear water." The name Wambighe, which approximates the Abenaki pronunciation, appeared on a 1715 map of the region.

UNH Trail *Chocorua Region*

A forestry camp operated by the University of New Hampshire (UNH) once was located near this trail to the ledges on Hedgehog Mountain.

Upper Ammonoosuc River *North Country*

Heading on the southeast side of the *Pilot Range,* this river flows north and then west around the range's north side to enter the *Connecticut River* near *Groveton.* See *Ammonoosuc (general).*

Upper Kimball Pond *Carter, Baldface Ranges*

See *Kimball Ponds.*

Valley Way *Northern Peaks, Great Gulf*   157

Connecting the *Appalachia* trailhead on U.S. Route 2 with the *Madison* Hut, this path was built by the White Mountains trailmaker J. Rayner Edmands in 1895–97 using parts of paths cut previously by trailmakers Laban M. Watson and Eugene B. Cook. It follows the valley of *Snyder Brook,* hence the name.

Vose Spur   (3,870 feet)   *Carrigain, Moat Regions*

This northeasterly spur of *Mount Carrigain* was named for Prof. George L. Vose of Paris, Maine, who assisted in the New Hampshire Geological Survey conducted by Prof. Charles H. Hitchcock.

Wachipauka Pond
Moosilauke Region

In the mountains west of Glencliff is this pond, whose name in Abenaki meant "mountain pond." In *Chatham* is a pond whose name is also *Mountain Pond,* though there in English.

Walden Trail
Chocorua, East Sandwich

This trail ascending *Mount Passaconaway* from Old Mast Road recalls Katherine Sleeper Walden; see *Sleeper Ridge.*

Walker Brook, Cascade, Ravine
Franconia, Twin, Willey Ranges

The origin of the name of these features on *Mount Lafayette*'s east side is obscure. It might be noted that an A. S. Walker of Boston in July 1855 climbed the old Glen Path to the summit of *Mount Washington barefooted,* but it is unlikely that a connection exists between the names and the tough-soled hiker.

Wamsutta Trail
Northern Peaks, Great Gulf

This path leading from the Mount Washington Auto Road to the *Great Gulf* Trail was named for the first of the six husbands of the Indian queen Weetamoo (see *Six Husbands Trail; Weetamoo Fall*).

Warren
Moosilauke Region

The town of Warren, nestled in the hills south of *Mount Moosilauke,* and Greenwich Village in New York City have one thing in common: a remarkable man named Peter Warren. Going to sea at fourteen, Peter by the time he was twenty-six was captain of his own ship, with seventy guns, and he continued to rise in position within the British Empire until he was eventually Sir Peter Warren, vice-admiral of the British Navy and Member of Parliament. The greatest achievement of his career, however, and the one that propelled him to greater fame, came in 1745 when he led a fleet of ships in the skillful capture of Louisbourg, Nova Scotia, a stronghold of the French, so strong it was called the "Dunkirk of America." Along the way in his career, Sir Peter Warren married a sister of the governor of New York, and he invested some of the "prize money" from his sea conquests in land that is now Greenwich Village and Washington Square on Manhattan Island. But his name is probably better remembered in this town in the White Mountains, which he probably never visited. The town was named for him when it was granted in 1764; Sir Peter Warren had died twelve years earlier.

Washington, Mount   (6,288 feet)
Mount Washington, Southern Ridges

The earliest names of this the highest peak in northeastern North America were simply descriptive. To the Abenaki-speaking peoples of the region, the peak was known as Kodaak Wadjo, meaning "summit of the highest mountain." It wasn't merely another peak to them, however, for they believed "amaji neowaska," or "bad spirit," dwelt here. The Indians also called the peak Agiochook, which has been interpreted to mean "the place of the Great Spirit." To some tribes, the peak and its neighbors were called Waumbekket-methna, meaning "snowy mountains." And the Algonquian Indians called the peak Waumbik, meaning "white rocks."

As for the mountain's English names, in 1628 the mariner Christopher Leavett referred to a mountain, likely Mount Washington, as the Christall Hill, and Governor Winthrop, writing in his journal in 1642 about Darby Field's ascent of the mountain that year, called the peak both the White Hill and the Sugarloaf.

In 1784, the same year Gen. George Washington retired from the Army to Mount Vernon, a scientific party led by Dr. Jeremy Belknap and including Dr. Manasseh Cutler climbed Mount Washington as part of their scientific explorations (Dr. Belknap himself did not reach the summit), and the name Mount Washington first appears in Dr. Cutler's manuscript reporting on the expedition. Later, Belknap used the name in the third volume of his *History of New Hampshire*, which appeared in 1792. This was the first appearance of the name Mount Washington in print. The first known appearance of the name Mount

Washington on a map came five years later, when a map by the German mapmaker Sotzmann labeled the mountain Washington B, the "B" standing for "berg," which is German for "mountain."

The name Mount Washington did not gain immediate acceptance, however; Dr. Jacob Bigelow, reporting on his 1816 expedition up the mountain, called it Mount Sugarloaf, although when Bigelow's party reached the summit they placed there a bottle containing a parchment that read, translated from the Latin:

> Preserve, oh traveler
> Whom the lightnings spare
> This fragile remembrance
> Lemuel Shaw
> Nathaniel Tucker
> Jacob Bigelow
> Francis Gray
> Francis Boott
> of Boston
> July second, A.D. 1816
> Mount Agiochook Conquered,
> We leave this behind.

Waternomee, Mount (approx. 3,500 feet)

Moosilauke Region

Formerly known as Blue Mountain, this peak just south of Kinsman Notch became known under its present name in 1876 when the AMC approved the use of the name Waternomee. Waternomee was an Abenaki chief killed in the massacre led by Capt. Thomas Baker in the spring of 1712 at what later became known as *Baker River*. The chief's name also appears on Waternomee Falls on Clifford Brook in *Warren*.

Waterville Valley

Waterville Valley Region

By an act of the New Hampshire General Court in 1967, Waterville Valley became the official name of this tiny town surrounded by high peaks. The mountains—*Tripyramid, Osceola, Tecumseh, Black, Sandwich,* and *Jennings*—were once known as the Waterville Haystacks. The area was first settled in the 1760s, and the village most likely took its name from the two rivers, the *Mad* and the *Swift*. The town was incorporated in 1829, and in 1830 Nathaniel Greeley settled here. In 1860 he built an inn and developed hiking and bridle trails for his guests (see *Greeley Brook, Ledges, Pond*). Modern development also has centered on the village's scenic location, trout fishing, and, since the late 1960s, skiing.

Watson Path   *Northern Peaks, Great Gulf*

This path to the summit of *Mount Madison* originally began at the Ravine House in *Randolph*, but following the construction of other trails it now begins at the Scar Trail. The path was named for its maker, Laban Watson, who laid it out in 1882. The Watson family had been in Randolph since Laban's grandfather, Stephen Watson, bought a farm on the Moose River (he later drowned in the river). Stephen's son, Abel, continued the farm, as did Laban, who turned it into the prosperous Ravine House, an important gathering place for trailmakers and hikers of the late 1800s. Watson guided and explored with William H. Peek, an association that lasted more than twenty-five years. J. Rayner Edmands often joined them, and they would spend their days building trails and exploring and making plans. Sometimes, when Eugene B. Cook was present, he would play his violin, and Chevalier Pychowska, a well-known musician, would often enter into the merrymaking. It was one of the most important—and most delightful—eras of White Mountains history.

Waumbek, Mount (3,020 feet)   *Northern Peaks, Great Gulf*

In some eastern Indian dialects, "waumbekket-methna" meant literally "snowy mountains," and in the Algonquin language "waumbik" meant "white rocks." From these comes the name of this the highest peak in the Pliny Range; *Pliny Major* was an early name for the summit.

Webster, Mount (3,910 feet)
Mount Washington, Southern Ridges

Topping the eastern bastion of *Crawford Notch* is this mountain, once called Notch Mountain but named as early as 1848 for the distinguished American statesman, lawyer, and native son of New Hampshire, Daniel Webster (1782–1852). Webster was no stranger to the White Mountains, and he praised them with his characteristic purple oratory. Yet he also was familiar with the less pleasant aspects of the White Mountains. One sultry morning in June he set out to climb *Mount Washington* with Ethan Allen Crawford as his guide. The weather was dour by the time they reached the top, and when they arrived Webster delivered the following address: "Mount Washington, I have come a long distance and toiled hard to reach your summit. Now you seem to give me a cold reception, for which I am extremely sorry, as I shall not be able to view the grand prospect which now lies before me—and nothing prevents but the uncomfortable atmosphere in which you reside." As if in response, the mountain's "atmosphere" pelted them with snow and sleet on their way down.

Weeks State Park, Mount (3,901 feet)   *North Country*

The Weeks family of *Lancaster* has had a long association with the White Mountains. Rev. Joshua Wingate Weeks was one of Lancaster's grantees in 1763, and roughly sixty years later John W. Weeks of Lancaster was among the leaders of the party that ascended the *Presidential Range* and named most of the major peaks for U.S. presidents. Still later, another John W. Weeks, born in Lancaster in 1860 and later a U.S. congressman and senator and Secretary of War during the administrations of Presidents Harding and Coolidge, was instrumental in the passage of the Weeks Act in 1911, which created the WMNF.

Secretary Weeks built a mansion atop a hill south of the village of Lancaster, and it remained in family ownership until 1941, when John's children presented it to the State of New Hampshire as a memorial to their father. The state turned it into a state park, where the principal attraction is the mansion offering a commanding view of the upper *Connecticut River* valley and several mountain ranges. John's son, Sinclair Weeks, a U.S. senator from Massachusetts and Secretary of Commerce during President Eisenhower's administration, came from Washington to dedicate the state park to his father.

Mount Weeks in the nearby *Pilot Range* was originally called Round Mountain because of its shape when viewed from the west, but now it, too, honors the Weeks family. Mount Weeks has three summits: North Peak, 3,901 feet; Middle Peak, 3,684 feet; and South Peak, 3,885 feet.

Weetamoo Fall   *Northern Peaks, Great Gulf*
Weetamoo Trail   *Chocorua, East Sandwich*

The name Weetamoo is a case study in how virtually all the many "Indian legends" of the White Mountains should be viewed, a contrast between myth-making and historical reality. The myth owes much to John Greenleaf Whittier, who, writing his poem "The Bridal of Penacook" from a remove of approximately 200 years, described the Indian maiden as:

> Child of the forest! Strong and free
> Slight-robed, with loosely flowing hair.

Whittier portrayed Weetamoo as the daughter of the great chief Passaconaway (see *Mount Passaconaway*) and a typical nineteenth-century tragic romantic heroine who sacrificed her life for her cold-hearted husband, Winnepurkit, sachem of Saugus. She perished when her canoe plunged over Amoskeag Falls on the Merrimack River.

Actually, there was indeed an Indian queen named Weetamoo and Passaconaway did indeed marry a daughter to a chief of Saugus. But the two don't match. The bride's name was Wanunchus, less euphonious than Weetamoo, (her husband's true name was Montowampate, less euphonious than Winnepurkit). And as for the historical Weetamoo, she was indeed a female chief but not of the Penacooks but of the Wampanoag tribe in what is now eastern Rhode Island and southern Massachusetts. Tradition says she had six husbands at different times (see *Six Husbands Trail*), the first of whom was Wamsutta (see *Wamsutta Trail*), brother of Metacomet, later better known as King Philip, whose uprising against the colonists was called King Philip's War. Weetamoo, loyal to her brother-in-law, died by drowning—like Whittier's Weetamoo. She was crossing a river fleeing a militia on August 6, 1676, six days before King Philip himself was killed. Their heads were cut off and displayed on poles.

With time, history and legend intermingle, and this process often is abetted by place names. The White Mountains features named after Weetamoo owe their names more to Whittier than to history. When the *Great Gulf* Trail was blazed in 1908, the beautiful falls below *Spaulding Lake* were named for her, doubtless in remembrance of Whittier's poem and not her role in King Philips War. Also, Weetamoo Fall on the West Branch of the *Peabody River* in the Great Gulf is named for her, as is Mount Weetamoo, 2,548 feet, in the *Sandwich Range* and Weetamoo Trail, a southern approach to *Mount Chocorua*.

Wentworths Location   *North Country*

New Hampshire's colonial governors, the Wentworths, who granted so many thousands of acres to others and thus named them, set aside this tract of wild North Country land next to the Maine border for their own purposes. They never made much use of it, however, and it was not incorporated until 1881, when the original name was retained.

West Bond (4,540 feet)   *Franconia, Twin, Willey Ranges*

See *Bond, Mount.*

Westside Trail   *Mount Washington, Southern Ridges*

Located on the west side of *Mount Washington*—hence the name—the Westside Trail connects the *Gulfside Trail* with the *Crawford Path*. It was built in part by J. Rayner Edmands.

Whiteface, Mount (4,015 feet)   *Chocorua, East Sandwich*

In 1820 a great landslide laid bare one face of this mountain, and many persons have thought this to be the origin of the name. With little doubt, an exposed face of bedrock is indeed responsible for the name, but the 1820 slide was only one of many that have occurred on the mountain, for the name Whiteface was mentioned in Dr. Jeremy Belknap's journal of 1784, and it appears on Philip Carrigain's map of 1816, both preceding the 1820 slide.

Whitefield   *Chocorua, East Sandwich*

In 1774, Gov. John Wentworth granted this town on the *Johns River* north of *Littleton*; Whitefield was the last New Hampshire town granted under English provincial rule. Although the name was originally listed as Whitefields, the name was changed to the present spelling when the town was incorporated in 1804. The name honors George Whitefield, the English evangelist who was very popular at the time. He had toured New England, and died at Exeter only four years before the granting of the town.

White Horse Ledge   *Carrigain, Moat Regions*

On the west bank of the *Saco River* opposite North Conway is a cliff much loved by rock climbers, on whose face is a light-colored patch resembling a dashing white horse, with a proud full tail. Legend has it that unmarried women of the area who hoped to change their status would look at the cliff, for an old New England tradition said that if a maid or widow saw a white horse and then counted to one hundred, the next man she saw would be her husband.

White Mountains

In all times, in all regions, people have called high snow-covered mountains "white." Dhaulagiri in the Himalayas, Craig Eyri in the Welsh mountains, Mont Blanc in the Alps—all translate to mean "white mountain." In North America, ranges named White Mountains are not only in northern New England but also in Arizona and eastern California-southwestern Nevada.

Whether the Indians had names for the entire mountain group here is unknown, though they called Mount Washington "waumbekketmethna," meaning "snowy or white mountain." The English mariner Christopher Leavett, writing in 1628 in his *A Voyage into New England,* called one of the mountains, most likely *Mount Washington,* the Christall Hill, a name later writers attributed to quartz crystals being found on the high peaks. Darby Field found some of these crystals when he ascended Mount Washington in 1642—he thought they were diamonds—but the name Crystal Hills was shortlived, for it was only thirty years later that the first mention of the name White Mountains appeared in print. In 1672 John Josselyn in his *New England Rarities Discovered* wrote of the Indians: "Ask them whither they go when they die, they will tell you, pointing with their finger, to heaven beyond the White Mountains."

Josselyn also wrote in his account: "The origin of all the great rivers in the countrie, the snow lies on the mountains the whole year excepting the month of August; the black flies are so numerous that a man cannot draw his breath but he will suck some of them in. Some suppose that the White Mountains were first raised by earthquakes, but they are hollow, as may be guessed by the resounding of the rain upon the level on the top."

This name, White Mountains, has been said to have been given first by mariners, for whom the distant white mountains were a landmark. As Ticknor wrote in his *White Mountains,* published in 1887, "they were a landmark and a mystery lifting their crowns of brilliant snow against the blue sky from October until June." Whether this is so or whether the English name translates an Indian name is not known, but no doubt exists as to the name's appropriateness.

White Mountains National Forest

By 1900 intensive logging and extensive forest fires had ravaged what had once been the pristine wilderness of the White Mountains. Viewing this with concern, conservation organizations and concerned individuals urged Congress to establish a White Mountains

Forest Preserve, and in 1911 the "Weeks Law" (see *Weeks State Park*) made possible federal purchase of forest lands at the heads of navigable streams east of the Mississipi; soon large tracts were acquired, though some private inholdings remain. Today the White Mountains National Forest encompasses 770,000 acres—47,000 acres in Maine, the rest in New Hampshire. The original objectives of preservation were enhanced in 1964 with the passage of the federal Wilderness Act; today the WMNF includes five wilderness areas: *Pemigewasset* (45,000 acres), *Presidential Range-Dry River* (27,380 acres), *Sandwich Range* (25,000 acres), *Great Gulf* (5,552 acres), and most recently, *Caribou Speckled* (approx. 12,000 acres).

Whitewall Brook, Mountain (3,410 feet)

Franconia, Twin, Willey Ranges

Whitewall Mountain forms the east flank of *Zealand* Notch and was named for a white rock face here. Whitewall Brook heads on the other side of the notch and flows south beneath the cliffs of Whitewall Mountain into the North Fork of the *Pemigewasset River*.

Wiggin Trail

Chocorua, East Sandwich

In 1895 Thomas S. Wiggin cut this trail to connect the Dicey Mill Trail with the *Blueberry Ledge* Trail on *Mount Whiteface*. The trail's nickname, "the Fire Escape," comes from the trail's steepness.

Wild Ammonoosuc River

Moosilauke Region

The Wild Ammonoosuc River heads on *Mount Moosilauke*'s northeast slopes and flows north then northwest to join the *Ammonoosuc River* between *Woodsville* and *Bath*. See *Ammonoosuc (general)*.

Wildcat Brook, River

Carter, Baldface Ranges

This brook heads on the east side of Wildcat Ridge and flows south to become the Wildcat River, eventually to enter the *Ellis River* at *Jackson*. The inspiration for the name has been forgotten; it is possible the brook took the name of the ridge where it heads. In 1988 Wildcat River was designated a National Wild and Scenic River.

Wildcat Mountain (4,422 feet) *Carter, Baldface Ranges*

Now the site of a ski area, this peak on the east side of *Pinkham Notch* was called East Mountain on early maps. By 1860, when Prof. Arnold Guyot's map was published, it was called by its present name, which most likely derived from a long-forgotten incident involving a wildcat on the mountain. It is said the mountain earlier had been called *Mount Hight,* but that name moved to another summit when Prof. Guyot gave the name Wildcat Mountain. Wildcat Mountain has five distinct summits, labeled alphabetically from east to west: A Peak, 4,422 feet; B Peak, 4,330 feet; C Peak, 4,298 feet; D Peak, 4,010 feet; and E Peak, 4,041 feet.

Wilderness Trail *Franconia, Twin, Willey Ranges*

This 8.9-mile trail connecting the *Kancamagus Highway* with Stillwater Junction is called the Wilderness Trail because it forms a central artery through the *Pemigewasset Wilderness.* The portion of the trail from the parking lot on the Kancamagus Highway to the wilderness boundary recently was changed to the Lincoln Woods Trail by the WMNF to reflect an historical name for the area, Lincoln Woods, but the rest of the trail retains the name Wilderness Trail.

Wild River *Carter, Baldface Ranges*

The Wild River heads on *Black Mountain*'s northeast slope north of *Jackson* and runs northeast to join the *Androscoggin River* at *Gilead,* Maine. The WMNF Wild River Campground is located at the confluence of this with Blue Brook. Describing a mountain stream as "wild" is relatively common throughout the U.S.; the White Mountains have not only this river but also the *Wild Ammonoosuc River.* The appropriateness of the name here is corroborated by a Benjamin Willey, who in 1856 wrote: "It is a child of the mountains; at times fierce, impetuous and shadowy, as the storms that howl around the bald heads of its parents, and bearing down everything in its path; then again, when subdued by long summer calms, murmuring gently in consonance with the breezy rustle of the trees." Later, timber barons also were to experience the river's wild unpredictability; major floods occurred in 1860, 1891, 1900, and 1903.

Willard, Mount (2,804 feet) *Franconia, Twin, Willey Ranges*

In 1844, Prof. Edward Tuckerman named this peak Mount Tom in honor of Thomas Crawford, a White Mountains guide and proprietor of the Crawford House. But just a few years later Thomas Crawford himself renamed it, this time to honor Joseph Willard of Boston, clerk of the Court of Common Pleas in Suffolk County. Willard was a guest at the Mount Crawford House, and together with Thomas Crawford he climbed the mountain named for him.

Willard Basin, Notch   *North Country*

According to local tradition, a man named Jonathan Willard came to the North Country from southern New Hampshire and became an eccentric recluse in the area later named for him. He was supposed to have been a cousin of Gov. Henry Hubbard, but he was content to live alone in the wilderness with only his dog, Pilot, for companionship. When the old hermit became infirm, his son came and took him back to civilization from whence he had fled. Local tradition also has it that nearby *Pilot Mountain* was named for Willard's dog, but, in fact, records show that the name predates the hermit, and that may also be true for Willard Notch and Basin, for these names appear on maps as early as 1816.

Willard Brook   *Speckled Mountain Region*

Heading on *Speckled Mountain* and flowing southeast, this takes its name from Samuel S. Willard, an early settler.

Willey, Mount (4,302 feet)   *Franconia, Twin, Willey Ranges*

In June 1826, members of the Samuel Willey family looked out from their home in *Crawford Notch* toward this mountain and witnessed a landslide that greatly frightened them. They thought, however, that such a slide was unlikely to occur again. They were tragically wrong.

Two months later, following heavy rains, a massive amount of earth, rocks, and trees descended from the mountain and wiped out the entire family. They undoubtedly sensed a slide was impending, for they fled their house, and most authorities believe they ran toward shelter in an outlying root cellar. They would have done better to have remained in the house, for a boulder behind the house caused the avalanche to split, and after the slide the house was the only building left standing.

The heavy rains caused severe flooding throughout the area, and soon friends and neighbors of the Willeys became concerned for their safety. A party that included Ethan Allen Crawford arrived at the

Willey homestead and found the family's cattle unmilked while all about lay in ruin and destruction. Searching amidst the rubble they found the bodies of Mr. and Mrs. Willey, two hired men, and two of the Willey's daughters. The bodies of three other children—one daughter and two sons—were never found. Ethan Allen Crawford later told his wife Lucy that he wept openly at the scene, only the second time tears had come to his eyes since he had achieved manhood.

Prof. Edward Tuckerman ascended the mountain in 1845, and he named the mountain for the family it had destroyed.

Wonalancet Village; Mount (2,800 feet)

Waterville Valley Region

Wonalancet, whose name means "governor," was a great Penacook Indian chief, the son and successor to the chief Passaconaway (see *Mount Passaconaway*). Despite his father's admonition to maintain peaceful relations with his white neighbors, often no easy task, Wonalancet in 1689 led an attack on Dover; pursued into Maine, he sued for peace in 1691, and soon thereafter most of the Penacooks left the White Mountains for Quebec.

The name for this mountain was suggested by the poet Lucy Larcom, a protégé of John Greenleaf Whittier and like him a great enthusiast of the White Mountains. The village of Wonalancet originally was called Birch Intervale, but in 1893 its name was changed to honor the chief. The mountain formerly was known as Toadback.

Woodstock

Moosilauke Region

The present name of this town on the *Pemigewasset River* is the third official name it has had during its history. When it was first granted in 1763 to Eli DeMerritt by Gov. Benning Wentworth it was called Peeling. The most likely origin of this name is that it came from an English town of that name. But because the grant consisted of sections pared off from surrounding towns, an apocryphal story says that DeMerritt named it because, "As this grant seems to be the peelings of all creation, let us call the township Peeling."

DeMerritt didn't settle in Peeling, and the lands were later re-granted. In 1771, Gov. John Wentworth renamed the town Fairfield, after Fairfield, Connecticut. But again settlement of the lands lagged, and the original name of Peeling persisted. This was not without opposition, however, and in 1813 a Rev. Benjamin Ropes preached a sermon—lasting until three o'clock in the afternoon—on the inappropriateness of the name Peeling. There was no reference in the Bible for it, he said; no town could prosper with such a name; and he urged the town's inhabitants to "peel it off."

Finally, in 1840, the name was changed again, this time to Woodstock, a name taken by many New England towns. It comes from the site of an historic palace in England that was also the setting for Sir Walter Scotts's novel *Woodstock*. Traces of the original settlement of Peeling, deserted by the Civil War, can still be found in the area's northern part.

Woodsville   *Connecticut Region*

Wood was responsible for the name of this town at the confluence of the *Connecticut* and *Ammonoosuc Rivers,* but not in the manner one might think. In 1830 a man named John L. Woods came from nearby Wells River, Vermont, to build a sawmill on the Ammonoosuc River, and from this beginning Woods prospered, eventually helping to make the town named for him the second most important railroad center in the state (Concord was the first). The village originally was called Governors Farm or Governors Reservation, because the Wentworths, in granting land, customarily reserved 500 acres for themselves to be assured of a future say in local government. All such lands were eventually returned to the towns.

Zealand

The origin of this name is obscure, but it appeared on early maps and records as New Zealand, suggesting some association with the islands in the South Pacific. The area was once described as the most beautiful virgin forest in the White Mountains, but then it was ravaged by fire. The virgin timber also attracted the nineteenth-century lumber baron James Everett Henry, and upon his logging operations grew a thriving community, complete with boardinghouses, a church, a school, a post office, a mill, and two train stations that at one time received as many as five trains a day to transport logs. Fire continued to plague the area, however, striking in 1886, 1897, and finally in 1903, the last fire destroying 84,000 acres of timber.

Henry knew the monetary value of White Mountains scenery, and when the Mount Washington House was being built, featuring a view of a beautiful maple-covered hillside that Henry owned, he informed the hotel's owners that unless they purchased the hillside from him at an inflated price he would log it and turn its trees into charcoal. The hotel people tried calling his bluff, but when Henry's crews began cutting and burning the trees they capitulated. Henry loved telling the story of his squeeze play, the price he received growing with each telling.

Whatever its origin, the name Zealand has spread to a number of features: Zealand Notch, Zealand Pond, Zealand Falls, Zealand River, Zealand Ridge and its highest point, Zealand Mountain, 4,260 feet, whereon is located Zeacliff, which in turn gave its name to Zeacliff Pond.

BIBLIOGRAPHY

Albany, New Hampshire, 1766–1966, Bicentennial Observance. Town of Albany, N.H., 1966.

Anderson, John, and Stearns Morse. *The Book of the White Mountains.* New York, 1930.

———. *AMC White Mountain Guide.* Boston: Appalachian Mountain Club, 1907–1992.

Beals, Charles Edwards, Jr. *Passaconaway in the White Mountains.* Boston, 1916.

Belknap, Jeremy. *History of New Hampshire.* 3 vols. Boston and Philadelphia, 1784–1792. Reprint. Hampton, N.H., 1973.

Belknap, Jeremy. "A New Map of New Hampshire." In vol. 1 of *History of New Hampshire.* Boston, 1791.

Bent, Allen H. "The Indians and the Mountains." *Appalachia* (June 1915): 257–71.

———. *A Bibliography of the White Mountains.* Boston, 1911. Reprint, edited by E. J. Hanrahan. Somersworth, N.H., 1971.

Berlin Historical Committee. *Berlin New Hampshire Centennial, 1829–1929.* Berlin, N.H., 1929.

Blanchard, Colonel, and Rev. Mr. Langdon, Geographer of His Majesty. *An Accurate Map of his Majesty's Province of New Hampshire in New England.* Portsmouth, N.H., 1761.

Bolnick, Bruce and Doreen. *Waterfalls of the White Mountains.* Woodstock, Vt., 1990.

Bond, George P. *A Map of the White Mountains.* 1853.

Bowles, Ella Shannon. *Let Me Show You New Hampshire.* New York, 1938.

Bryant, W. C., ed. *Picturesque America, Part Seven.* New York, 1872.

Burt, Frank H. "The Nomenclature of the White Mountains." *Appalachia* (December 1915): 359–90.

———. "The Nomenclature of the White Mountains II." *Appalachia* (June 1915): 261–68.

————. "The White Mountains Forty Years Ago." *Appalachia* (December 1916): 37–49.

Carrigain, Philip. *A Map of New Hampshire*. Concord, 1816.

Child, Hamilton, comp. *Grafton County Gazeteer, 1709–1886*. Syracuse, N.Y., 1886.

Choate, Malcolm C., Miriam Underhill, and Robert L. M. Underhill. *Kearsarge: On the History of the Name as Applied to the Mountain in Carrroll County, N.H.* Report to the Appalachian Mountain Club, 1957.

Conrad, Justus. *The Town of Woodstock and its Scenic Beauties*. Littleton, N.H.

Crawford, Lucy. *Lucy Crawford's History of the White Mountains*. Edited by Stearns Morse. Hanover, N.H., 1966. First published as *White Hills*. 1846.

Cross, George N. *Randolph Old and New: Its Ways and Its By-ways*. Town of Randolph, N.H., 1924.

————. "Randolph Yesterdays." *Appalachia* (December 1916): 49–58.

Cutter, Louis F. "The Edmands Paths and their Builder." *Appalachia* (August 1921): 124–140.

————. *Decisions of the U.S. Board on Geographic Names, 1890–1990*. Reston, Va.: U.S. Geological Survey, Branch of Geographic Names.

Drake, Samuel Adams. *The Heart of the White Mountains*. New York, 1882.

Dummer Bicentennial Committee. *History of Dummer, New Hampshire, 1773–1973*. Littleton, N.H., 1973.

Eastman, Samuel C. *The White Mountain Guidebook*. Concord, N.H., 1858–1884.

Evans, George Hill. *Handbook of Cold River Valley and Adjacent Territory*. Chatham, N.H.: Chatham Trails Assoc., 1932.

Farmer, John, and Jacob B. Moore. *A Gazeteer of the State of New Hampshire*. Concord, N.H., 1823.

Fay, Charles E. "The Annual Address of the President: Our Geographical Nomenclature." *Appalachia* (June 1882): 1–3.

Federal Writers Project. *New Hampshire, A guide to the Granite State*. Boston: Works Progress Administration, 1938.

————. *Geographic Names Information System Alphabetical Listing—New Hampshire, 1990*. Reston, Va.: U.S. Geological Survey, Branch of Geographic Names.

Goodrich, Nathaniel L. *The Waterville Valley: A Story of a Resort in the New Hampshire Mountains*. Lunenburg, Vt., 1952.

Gore, Effie K., and Eva A. Speare, comps. *New Hampshire Folk Talkes*. New Hampshire Federation of Women's Clubs, 1832. Revised. Littleton, N.H., 1964.

Hammond, Otis G. *A Checklist of New Hampshire History*. Concord, N.H., 1925. Reprint, edited by E. J. Hanrahan. Somersworth, N.H., 1971.

————. *Handbook of North American Indians*. Vol. 15. Edited by William C. Sturtevant. Washington, D.C.: Smithsonian Institution, 1978.

Hart, Warren W. "Timothy Nash." *Appalachia* (June 1919): 383–90.

Hitchcock, Charles H. "Map of New Hampshire." Atlas accompanying *Report on the Geology of New Hampshire*. New York, 1878.

Holland, Samuel. *A Topographical Map of the State of New Hampshire*. London, 1784.

Horne, Ruth B. D. *Conway Through the Years and Whither*. Conway, N.H., 1963.

Horton, Louise S., Elizabeth H. Underhill, and Eleanor D. Deal. *Piermont, New Hampshire (1764–1947)*. Bradford, Vt.

Huden, John C. *Indian Place Names of New England*. New York, 1962.

Hunt, Elmer Munson. *New Hampshire Town Names and Whence They Came*. Peterborough, 1970.

Hunt, Elmer Munson. "The Origin of Some New Hampshire Mountain Names." *Historical New Hampshire* (April 1955): 1–28.

Joy, Thelma, and Ann Georgia, eds. *Woodstock, New Hampshire, Celebrates 200 Years*. North Woodstock, N.H.

Kilbourne, Frederick W. *Chronicles of the White Mountains*. Boston, 1916.

King, Thomas Starr. *The White Hills: Their Legends, Landscape, and Poetry*. Boston, 1859.

Leavitt, Franklin. *A Map of the White Mountains*. Boston, 1852.

Lehr, Frederic B. *Carroll, New Hampshire: The First 200 Years, 1772–1972*. Littleton, N.H., 1972.

Leitch, Barbara A. *A Concise Dictionary of Indian Tribes of North America*. Algonac, Mich., 1979.

Lewis, Samuel. *Map of the State of New Hampshire*. Philadelphia, 1974.

———. *Arrowsmith and Lewis New and Elegant General Atlas*. 1805.

Merrill, Georgia Drew. *History of Carroll County*. Boston, 1889. Reprint. Somersworth, N.H., 1971.

———. *History of Coös County, New Hampshire*. Boston, 1888. Reprint. Somersworth, N.H., 1972.

Milan Bicentennial History Committee. *Historical Notes and Pictures of Milan, New Hampshire, 1771–1971*, Littleton, N.H., 1971.

Mudge, John T. B., *The White Mountains: Names, Places, and Legends*. Etna, N.H.: The Durand Press, 1992.

Nilsen, Kim R. *A History of Whitefield, New Hampshire, 1774–1974*. Whitefield, N.H., 1974.

Oakes, William. *Scenery of the White Mountains*. Boston, 1848.

O'Kane, Walter Collins. *Trails and Summits of the White Mountains*. Boston, 1925.

Olsen, John. "Pinkham Woods." *Appalachia* (December 1946): 225–30.

Peabody, Dean, Jr. "The Evolution of the AMC Hut." *Appalachia* (December 1931): 432–37.

Poole, Ernest. *The Great White Hills of New Hampshire*. New York, 1946.

Powers, Rev. Grant. *Historical Sketches of the Discovery, Settlement, and Progress of Events in the Coös County and Vicinity, Principally Included Between the Years 1754 and 1785.* Haverhill, N.H., 1841. Reprint. 1880.

Proctor, Mary A. *The Indians of the Winnepesaukee and Pemigewasset Valleys.* Franklin, 1930.

Randall, Peter. *Mount Washington: A Guide and Short History.* Hanover, N.H., 1974.

Rutherford, Phillip R. *The Dictionary of Maine Place-Names.* Freeport, Me., 1970.

Slosson, Annie Trumbull. *Fishin' Jimmy.* New York, 1889.

Spaulding, John H. *Historical Relics of the White Mountains.* Boston, 1855.

Stark Bicentennial Committee. *History of Stark, New Hampshire, 1774–1974.* Littleton, N.H., 1974.

State Papers. *N.H. Town Charters* Vols. 1 and 2. Edited by Albert Stillman Batchellor. Concord, N.H., 1895.

Swan, Bradford F. "The Earliest Map of the White Mountains." *Appalachia* (1965): 386–88.

Sweetser, Moses F. *The White Mountains, A Handbook for Travelers.* Boston, 1876.

Thompson, Jeanette R. *History of the Town of Stratford, New Hampshire, 1773–1925.* Concord, N.H., 1925.

Tuckerman, Frederick. "Early Visits to the White Mountains." *Appalachia* (August 1921): 111–27.

Upham, Warren. "Unnamed Mountains Between Mt. Hancock and Scar Ridge." *Appalachia* (February 1878): 252–58.

———. *White Mountain National Forest* (map). Milwaukee, Wisc.: White Mountain National Forest, U.S. Forest Service, 1972. Revised 1981.

———. *The White Mountains: Place and Perceptions.* Edited by Donald D. Keyes. Hanover, N.H.: University Press of New England, 1980.

Wight, Denman B. *The Androscoggin River Valley: Gateway to the White Mountains.* Rutland, Vt., 1967.

Willey, Benjamin G. *Incidents in White Mountain History.* Boston, 1856.

Willey, Wilbur. *West of Littleton.*

Woodbury, Elmer E. *Historical Narrative of "Lost River" and "Kinsman Notch."* Littleton, N.H., n.d.

UNIVERSITY PRESS OF NEW ENGLAND
publishes books under its own imprint and is the publisher for Brandeis University Press, Brown University
Press, University of Connecticut, Dartmouth College,
Middlebury College Press, University of New Hampshire,
University of Rhode Island, Tufts University, University
of Vermont, and Wesleyan University Press.

Library of Congress Cataloging-in-Publication Data

Julyan, Robert Hixson.
    Place names of the White Mountains / by Robert and Mary
Julyan.
        p.   cm.
    ISBN 0–87451–638–2
    1. Names, Geographical—White Mountains (N.H. and Me.)   2. White
Mountains (N.H. and Me.)—Geography.   I. Julyan, Mary.   II. Title.
F41.2.J85   1993
917.42'2'003—dc20   93–13606
♾